S. Hrg. 113–180

EXAMINING PROSPECTSFOR DEMO-CRATIC REFORM AND ECONOMIC RECOVERY IN ZIMBABWE

HEARING

BEFORE THE

SUBCOMMITTEE ON AFRICAN AFFAIRS

OF THE

COMMITTEE ON FOREIGN RELATIONS UNITED STATES SENATE

ONE HUNDRED THIRTEENTH CONGRESS

FIRST SESSION

———

JUNE 18, 2013

———

Printed for the use of the Committee on Foreign Relations

Available via the World Wide Web: http://www.gpo.gov/fdsys/

U.S. GOVERNMENT PRINTING OFFICE

86–777 PDF   WASHINGTON : 2014

For sale by the Superintendent of Documents, U.S. Government Printing Office
Internet: bookstore.gpo.gov   Phone: toll free (866) 512–1800; DC area (202) 512–1800
Fax: (202) 512–2104   Mail: Stop IDCC, Washington, DC 20402–0001

COMMITTEE ON FOREIGN RELATIONS

ROBERT MENENDEZ, New Jersey, *Chairman*

BARBARA BOXER, California
BENJAMIN L. CARDIN, Maryland
ROBERT P. CASEY, Jr., Pennsylvania
JEANNE SHAHEEN, New Hampshire
CHRISTOPHER A. COONS, Delaware
RICHARD J. DURBIN, Illinois
TOM UDALL, New Mexico
CHRISTOPHER MURPHY, Connecticut
TIM KAINE, Virginia

BOB CORKER, Tennessee
JAMES E. RISCH, Idaho
MARCO RUBIO, Florida
RON JOHNSON, Wisconsin
JEFF FLAKE, Arizona
JOHN McCAIN, Arizona
JOHN BARRASSO, Wyoming
RAND PAUL, Kentucky

DANIEL E. O'BRIEN, *Staff Director*
LESTER E. MUNSON III, *Republican Staff Director*

SUBCOMMITTEE ON AFRICAN AFFAIRS

CHRISTOPHER A. COONS, Delaware, *Chairman*

BENJAMIN L. CARDIN, Maryland
JEANNE SHAHEEN, New Hampshire
RICHARD J. DURBIN, Illinois
TOM UDALL, New Mexico

JEFF FLAKE, Arizona
JOHN McCAIN, Arizona
JOHN BARRASSO, Wyoming
RAND PAUL, Kentucky

(II)

CONTENTS

EXAMINING PROSPECTS FOR DEMOCRATIC REFORM AND ECONOMIC RECOVERY IN ZIMBABWE

TUESDAY, JUNE 18, 2013

U.S. SENATE,
SUBCOMMITTEE ON AFRICAN AFFAIRS,
COMMITTEE ON FOREIGN RELATIONS,
Washington, DC.

The subcommittee met, pursuant to notice, at 10:07 a.m., in room SD–419, Dirksen Senate Office Building, Hon. Christopher A. Coons (chairman of the subcommittee) presiding.

Present: Senators Coons, and Flake.

OPENING STATEMENT OF HON. CHRISTOPHER A. COONS, U.S. SENATOR FROM DELAWARE

Senator COONS. Good morning. I would like to call this hearing of the African Affairs Subcommittee to order. Today we will focus our attention on Zimbabwe, a country with abundant natural resources, human resources, fertile land, and a capable and enterprising population. Zimbabwe should be driving growth and prosperity in southern Africa, but today instead, in the 33 years since independence, Zimbabweans' prospects have become increasingly bleak, having reached a low point in 2008 when the economy nearly collapsed and having slowly made modest progress since.

It is no coincidence the economic collapse came at the same time as a significant decrease in respect for democratic principles and the rule of law and harsh crackdowns on free expression, civil society, and the news media.

Zimbabweans will go to the polls at some point later this year for the first elections under their newly ratified constitution, and the preparation for and conduct of these elections will be an important indicator of whether Zimbabwe can and will realize its great economic and democratic potential.

I would like to welcome my partner on the subcommittee, Ranking Member Senator Jeff Flake of Arizona, who brings with him considerable personal insight on Zimbabwe from his time spent in that country, and I look forward to continuing to work with him to advance our shared interests in good governance, economic growth, and security throughout sub-Saharan Africa.

I would like to welcome our distinguished witnesses today: Don Yamamoto, Acting Assistant Secretary of State for Africa; Earl Gast, the Assistant Administrator for Africa at USAID, on our first panel, as well as our second panel to follow them: Dewa Mahvinga, senior researcher at Human Rights Watch; Mark Schneider, senior VP at International Crisis Group; and Todd Moss, the vice president for programs and senior fellow at the Center for Global Development. I look forward to hearing your insights and thank you for being here.

Relations between the United States and Zimbabwe are guided by our shared aspiration for democratic and humanitarian values. The United States, though, has in recent years had to impose targeted travel and financial sanctions against individuals and businesses in Zimbabwe who have been engaged in persistently undermining democratic institutions. But we have in other ways remained a steadfast partner to the people of Zimbabwe. We have provided, over the dozen years since 2001, nearly $1.5 billion in support, much of which has helped address ongoing health and humanitarian needs of millions of regular Zimbabweans. The fiscal year 2014 request, if I am not mistaken, is for $135 million.

Although providing this aid has been in the broadest sense the right thing to do, better governance and respect for rule of law in Zimbabwe would open the door to a stronger and different kind of partnership with the United States, one that leverages our resources and expertise more strategically to expand trade and investment and cooperatively approach vital regional challenges. Zimbabweans need not be destined for prolonged dependence on foreign aid.

The upcoming elections offer Zimbabweans a critical chance to show their commitment to their new constitution, which limits Executive power and protects civil rights, and to build on the stabilization of the economy ushered in under the coalition government.

SADC members have a critical and challenging role to play in supporting the elections and in holding Zimbabwe accountable to the standards it set in its new constitution. I am concerned from recent reports that the Zimbabwean Government is not working in good faith with SADC and other international partners to ensure these elections will be free and fair, especially considering the lengths to which President Mugabe and his ZANU–PF loyalists went to preserve power in the 2008 elections. I am alarmed by the uptick in targeted harassment and intimidation of civil society leaders and human rights defenders who are seeking to ensure a free, fair, and open election. Activists such as human rights lawyer Beatrice Mtetwa have been harassed and arrested and leaders of security forces have in some recent instances been openly partisan and acting to suppress democratic expression.

Today's hearing will look at the tools the United States could effectively deploy to support the upcoming elections and post-electoral reforms, to support increased respect for human rights and rule of law and mutually beneficial relations between our countries. I look forward to continuing my own engagement with SADC members and the administration following on this hearing and to make recommendations based on the advice we hear from our five witnesses today.

With that, I turn it over to Senator Flake for his opening statement.

OPENING STATEMENT OF HON. JEFF FLAKE,
U.S. SENATOR FROM ARIZONA

Senator FLAKE. Well, thank you, Mr. Chairman. Thanks for arranging this hearing, and thank you to the witnesses. I look forward to the testimony.

As you mentioned, I have a personal interest here. I spent a good deal of time in Zimbabwe in 1982–1983, back when there was great hope that things would turn out better than they have. As the chairman said, the purpose of this hearing is to see what we can do, what constructive role can the United States play to ensure a better future than it looks like we are in for right now. We will see if these election dates will hold and, if they do, if the outcome will be respected and will be credible.

So look forward to the testimony and thank you again for coming.

Senator COONS. Thank you, Senator Flake.

I would now like to turn to our first panel, starting with Ambassador Yamamoto and then followed by Assistant Administrator Gast.

Ambassador.

STATEMENT OF HON. DONALD YAMAMOTO, ACTING ASSIST-ANT SECRETARY OF STATE FOR AFRICAN AFFAIRS, BUREAU OF AFRICAN AFFAIRS, U.S. DEPARTMENT OF STATE, WASH-INGTON, DC

Senator COONS. Thank you very much, Senator Coons and Senator Flake. And thank you very much for having this hearing on Zimbabwe, and also for your deep concern and also great work on this important issue. For the sake of time, I would like to submit a longer version for the record.

I would like to start off by noting that in the past year we have made engagements to move the Zimbabwe Government toward a much more open, free, fair, and transparent electoral process. In that regards, former U.N. Ambassador Andrew Young delivered a letter to President Mugabe from Secretary Kerry outlining the opportunities for normalized relations.

Let me just say that Zimbabwe now is at the crossroads. Either it is going to go back to 1999 when it refused to pay for loans and concede to debt relief, or is it going to go forward in the progress that has been made in the last few years? We can see the progress. HIV–AIDS infection rates have fallen to below 15 percent. That is about half of what it was in 1999. The United States has helped them to meet the issues of cholera and tuberculosis and also further the issues on HIV–AIDS issues.

The other issue, too, is that the MDC-managed finances have helped to bring down inflation rates to almost zero, but also to have economic growth in the last 4 years which is about 5 percent. We are also looking at independent newspapers increasing, commercial radios. Outflows of economic migrants into South Africa and to other areas has decreased. Trade is up with the United States from about $100 million to $160 million.

But these all stand to be sacrificed if these upcoming elections are not free, fair, open, and transparent. We share your deep concerns about the trendlines that we are seeing. But the recent statements by SADC to have Zimbabwe go back to the constitutional process, the African Union sending observers, I think we are going to continue to work with all the stakeholders to ensure that this happens.

But if it does not, if we do have a problem of regression on the part of Zimbabwe, then I think we can look at other issues and other areas in which we can make a difference for the people of Zimbabwe. Again, this is at a crossroads for Zimbabwe, the future progress for the people of Zimbabwe or to the past.

Thank you very much.

[The prepared statement of Ambassador Yamamoto follows:]

PREPARED STATEMENT BY ACTING ASSISTANT SECRETARY DONALD YAMAMOTO

Chairman Coons, Ranking Member Flake, and distinguished members of the committee, thank you for holding this hearing on Zimbabwe. Thank you also for affording me the privilege of testifying before you about this very important country at this critical juncture. It is my honor to have this opportunity to speak with you and our other assembled guests here today about the Department of State's work in Zimbabwe. We appreciate the deep interest of this committee in Zimbabwe over the years, and we are pleased to work closely with Members of Congress in support of our national interests in Zimbabwe and the region.

After nearly 5 years under Zimbabwe's unity government, 2013 began as a year of promise and opportunity for Zimbabwe. In February, President Mugabe's ZANU–PF party and the MDC parties led by Morgan Tsvangirai and Welshman Ncube agreed on a draft constitution. In March, Zimbabwe held a peaceful referendum in which the Zimbabwean people overwhelmingly approved the draft constitution and, on May 22, President Mugabe signed Zimbabwe's new constitution into law.

The June 15 communique issued by the Southern African Development Community (SADC) called for the parties in Zimbabwe's unity government to seek more time to complete important reforms and create a conducive environment for peaceful, credible elections. Too short a timeline would risk undermining the careful work of SADC to build a framework for peaceful, credible, transparent elections and to ensure necessary reforms are in place.

These elections present an important opportunity for Zimbabwe to improve its relationship with the United States by holding elections that are regarded as peaceful, credible, and transparent by a broad range of international observers. Former U.S. Ambassador to the U.N. and civil rights leader, Andrew Young, recently delivered a letter to President Mugabe from Secretary Kerry outlining this opportunity. As elections approach, however, reports indicate that elements within Zimbabwean political parties and government security agencies have already begun efforts to intimidate voters and illicitly shape the outcome of the elections.

This includes a troubling trend of arrests, detentions, and harassment of organizations and individuals working on human rights, electoral assistance, and related issues. The chilly reception offered to a partial U.N. Electoral Needs Assessment Mission (after all but one member of the delegation was denied entry into Zimbabwe), Zimbabwean hardliners' persistence in brushing off calls for a broad range of international election observers, and ZANU–PF's insistence on the removal of all sanctions rather than recognizing good faith efforts to ease some restrictions constitute obstacles to the conditions that we feel are necessary for warming relations between the United States and Zimbabwe. Influential officials within the Zimbabwean Government and the Zimbabwean defense and security sectors who benefit from the perpetuation of the status quo remain the most vocal critics of further engagement with the "West."

The Government of Zimbabwe now faces a key decision point. Zimbabwe must decide whether it will support a credible electoral process, or continue to repress its people and isolate itself from the international community. The 2011 Southern African Development Community's (SADC) Roadmap and Zimbabwe's new constitution outline key reforms focused on voter education and registration, inspection of voters' rolls, media reform, security sector reform, freedom of assembly and association. We are concerned that holding elections without providing adequate time for voter registration, inspection of voters' rolls, other needed electoral and democratic reforms—particularly reforms of the Public Order and Security Act, media reforms, and security sector reforms—will put the credibility of the outcome at risk.

The United States shares the same fundamental interest as the people of Zimbabwe: a stable, peaceful, democratic Zimbabwe that reflects the will of her people and provides for their needs. U.S. support for human rights and democracy groups contributed to the success of the long and difficult development of Zimbabwe's new constitution. The U.S. also supported Zimbabwe's progress in attaining universal coverage for antiretroviral treatment, reducing the HIV/AIDS prevalence to just under 15 percent and extending the quality and reach of Zimbabwe's health care system. U.S. development assistance in smallholder farming has improved the lives of tens of thousands of everyday Zimbabweans, and U.S. support to the quasi-governmental statistics and economic research institutions, as well as nongovernmental organizations, has fostered a more disciplined approach to evidence-based fiscal and agriculture policy development in Zimbabwe.

In May, following the peaceful and credible constitutional referendum, and as a means of demonstrating the sincerity of our intent to work toward normalizing relations should Zimbabwe make progress consolidating its democratic institutions, the administration eased restrictions on two Zimbabwean banks—the Agricultural Development Bank of Zimbabwe and the Infrastructure Development Bank of Zimbabwe. Both remain on the Office of Foreign Assets Control's (OFAC) list of Specially Designated Nationals (SDN List), despite the issuance of a General License by OFAC allowing Americans to conduct transactions with those banks. As part of our regular review of U.S. targeted sanctions, we also removed eight individuals and one entity designated under the Zimbabwe sanctions program from the SDN list. Some of the individuals are recently deceased, but others have left their positions in the Zimbabwean Government or are now using positions of influence to effect positive change; 113 individuals and 70 entities remain sanctioned under the Zimbabwe program today.

In an effort to leverage SADC's consistent position that elections in Zimbabwe should be conducted properly rather than expediently, we in Washington and our Ambassadors in the field have been working to highlight and reinforce key U.S. policies on Zimbabwe, including strong support for SADC as the guarantor of the Global Political Agreement (GPA) and creator of the roadmap charting the reforms to which the unity government has committed. The people of Zimbabwe deserve the full and complete enactment of the reforms called for in the GPA, the SADC Roadmap, and the new constitution prior to elections. An environment free of political intimidation and violence, and the inclusion of a broad range of international observers, are essential for credible elections. Led by SADC, a robust contingent of election observers would play a central role in verifying that the credibility of the upcoming election and Zimbabwe's ability to live up to international electoral standards. The absence of local and international observers would detract from the credibility of the electoral process.

We are also profoundly troubled by the lack of transparency within the diamond sector and the possibilities for illicit diamond sales in Zimbabwe. We are concerned about ongoing reports that diamond mining entities in Zimbabwe are being exploited by people in senior government and military positions for personal gain, that revenues from those enterprises are being diverted for partisan activities that undermine democracy, and that proceeds from diamond sales are enriching a few individuals and not the Treasury and people of Zimbabwe. The Zimbabwean people deserve to benefit from Zimbabwe's diamond fields and the many millions of carats (and dollars) that they likely hold.

Giving all Zimbabweans the opportunity to choose their government this year, in peaceful, credible, and transparent elections, will help ensure a democratic, prosperous future for Zimbabwe. The United States Government has made it clear that we deeply respect the sovereign will of the Zimbabwean people, and that we will work with any government chosen in such elections.

We are prepared to consider steps to further roll back sanctions and expand trade and investment between our countries. However, as a necessary first step, Zimbabwe must first hold elections that are peaceful, credible, transparent, and truly reflective of the will of the Zimbabwean people, and which are verified as such by a broad range of international observers. Thank you for providing me the opportunity to speak with your committee today. I welcome any questions you may have at this time.

Senator COONS. Thank you, Ambassador.
Assistant Administrator Gast.

STATEMENT OF HON. EARL GAST, ASSISTANT ADMINISTRATOR FOR AFRICA, BUREAU FOR AFRICA, UNITED STATES AGENCY FOR INTERNATIONAL DEVELOPMENT, WASHINGTON, DC

Mr. GAST. Good morning, Chairman Coons and Ranking Member Flake. Thank you for the opportunity to speak with you today. I appreciate your continued interest in how United States policies and assistance programs can help build a peaceful and stable democracy in which prosperity is available to all in Zimbabwe. I would also like to thank Acting Assistant Secretary Yamamoto for his leadership on this issue.

The negotiated resolution to Zimbabwe's violent electoral dispute in 2008 brought with it an opportunity for the consolidation of democratic institutions and improved systems of governance in Zimbabwe. A government of national unity agreed on a roadmap to achieve sustained political stability through stronger democratic processes. Broadly, the General Political Agreement, or the GPA, required the unity government to draft a new constitution, enhance basic reforms and freedoms, and reform Zimbabwe's security sector before the next elections, because the steps taken before and after election day are just as important as the election day itself.

However, recently, on the 13th of June, President Mugabe issued a proclamation fixing July 31 as the day for harmonized Presidential, parliamentary, and local government elections. Though he claims his action was compulsory due to a constitutional court ruling, the ruling itself is highly questionable as it does not take into account the GPA's requirements, which are necessary for credible elections.

The absence of transparent and accountable preelectoral processes will cast doubt regarding the legitimacy of the election results. At the same time, civil society leaders are facing increasing incidences of intimidation and harassment. Restrictions on media freedoms and public meetings, particularly in rural areas, are common. Furthermore, whether as a result of insufficient resources or political will, government attempts to provide even basic information on the voter registration process have been inadequate. This is as we are entering the second week of voter registration.

As preparations progress, USAID continues to provide support where possible in an effort to address or at least mitigate these challenges. This support has three core pillars. One is empowering citizen participation in the elections. The second is supporting observation in the electoral process. Then the third is supporting credible elections administration.

The first pillar emphasizes access to information as key to catalyzing participation of citizens, particularly women and youth, both groups of which have been underrepresented in elections previously. At USAID-supported youth clubs, young men and women have consistently expressed concern about the unmet need for basic information, particularly outside of urban areas. In response, a dynamic group of young partners has designed a groundbreaking voter response and a mobilization campaign that is broadcast on weekly radio programs and through social media outlets. So it is for the first time that we are seeing Zimbabwean youth very much engaged in debating issues that are related to the elections.

Given the history of violence associated with Zimbabwe's past elections, peace-building and reconciliation are critical, and we are seeing faith-based organizations stepping up and playing a critical role. We are seeing large-scale peace rallies and in those rallies representatives from across the political spectrum are very much involved in this.

The second pillar of USAID programs focuses on observation of the electoral process in accordance with the principles of SADC, which is the regional organization that has been monitoring the implementation of the GPA. USAID and other donors are funding domestic observation efforts, but avenues to support international observation are limited at this point.

Despite calls from the international community and Zimbabwean civil society for long-term international or regional observers to document the preelection environment, the electoral law does not provide a mechanism for accrediting long-term observers. We feel having long-term observers in place would absolutely be essential to help ensure that we have credible elections.

The third pillar of our work is supporting elections administration. We are engaged with civil society and others to provide evidence-based research and information on best practices in the region. The goal is to provide this information to key stakeholders, including parliamentarians and members of the Zimbabwe Electoral Commission, to ensure that legal and regulatory frameworks provide a foundation for transparent and credible elections.

Our overall assistance, be it in health or be it in economic growth, support—our assistance supports these three pillars. We feel by providing basic services for Zimbabwe's citizens we not only meet immediate needs, but also demonstrate that better governance can lead to better lives. We have provided substantial support to combat the spread of HIV–AIDS, while other efforts are increasing food security, which is now a critical issue for Zimbabwe, and we are working to improve Zimbabwe's business environment to help attract private investment.

We will continue to prioritize human rights and conflict mitigation and management activities as we move to the elections and beyond the elections.

Thank you for your support.

[The prepared statement of Mr. Gast follows:]

PREPARED STATEMENT OF ASSISTANT ADMINISTRATOR EARL GAST

Chairman Coons, Ranking Member Flake, and members of the subcommittee, I would like to thank you for the opportunity to speak with you today. I appreciate your continued interest in how U.S. policies and assistance programs can help Zimbabweans build a peaceful and stable democracy in which prosperity is available to all. I would also like to thank the Acting Assistant Secretary for Africa at the Department of State for his leadership on this issue.

The negotiated resolution to Zimbabwe's violent electoral dispute in 2008 brought with it an opportunity for the consolidation of democratic institutions and improved systems of governance in Zimbabwe. A Government of National Unity (GNU) was formed, composed of Zimbabwe's then-ruling party, Zimbabwe African National Union-Patriotic Front (ZANU–PF), and the two factions of the former opposition party, Movement for Democratic Change (MDC)–MDC–T (Tsvangirai) and MDC–N (Ncube). Together, the parties of the unity government agreed on a roadmap to achieve sustained political stability through stronger democratic processes. Broadly, the General Political Agreement (GPA) required that the GNU would draft a new constitution, enhance basic freedoms (including media), and reform Zimbabwe's security sector before the next elections were held.

USAID has strongly supported the unity government's efforts to implement the GPA, including the development of a new constitution, which was adopted in May 2013. The U.S. Government worked with the Zimbabwean Parliament and civil society to ensure that the new constitution would expand protections under the bill of rights and enhance gender equity provisions. USAID support for civil society activities culminated in an awareness-raising program highlighting the need for youth to peacefully participate in the March 16 referendum through which a record voter turnout overwhelmingly endorsed the new constitution.

Yet challenges remain. On May 31, the Constitutional Court ruled that elections must be held by the end of July, and on June 13 President Mugabe issued a Presidential decree declaring July 31 the date of elections. However, little progress has been made on the other key reforms identified in the GPA—most notably, media and security sector reforms—and it is unlikely that full implementation of the agreement could occur by July 31. The constitution includes strict requirements that must be fulfilled during the preelection period, including voter registration and inspection of the voter role, and candidate primaries. It also requires that the Electoral Law be updated by the Parliament to reflect changes in the constitution before an election date can be set—procedures that were not respected in President Mugabe's decree. The absence of clear, governing law may give rise to challenges in the post-election period and underscores the need to follow an agreed upon, detailed election roadmap.

The requirements included in the GPA are important because progress made in reforming these sectors is necessary for a credible election. The absence of transparent and accountable preelectoral processes will cast doubt regarding the legitimacy of the election results. Civil society leaders are facing increasing incidences of intimidation and harassment. Restrictions on media freedoms and public meetings—particularly in rural areas—are common. Furthermore, whether as a result of insufficient resources or political will, government attempts to provide basic information on the voter registration process have been inadequate. The steps taken before and after election day are just as, if not more, important than the election day itself.

The new chair of the Zimbabwe Electoral Commission (ZEC) has demonstrated commitment to addressing many of these shortcomings and is reaching out to key stakeholders, including political party leaders and civil society, to improve the process. Previously, it cost $30,000 to obtain a comprehensive copy of the country's voter rolls—a sum out of reach of political parties and civil society. As a result of her direct efforts, the cost has dropped to $5,000. These efforts could produce legitimate reforms to begin to address the question of the Zimbabwean Government's ability and will to conduct free and fair registration and electoral processes.

As preparations progress, USAID continues to provide support where possible in an effort to address these challenges. This support has three core pillars: empowering citizen participation in the elections, observing the election process, and supporting credible election administration.

The first pillar emphasizes access to information as key to catalyzing the participation of citizens—particularly women and youth. At USAID-supported youth clubs, young men and women have consistently expressed concern about the unmet need for basic information, particularly outside of urban areas. In response, a dynamic group of young partners designed a groundbreaking voter mobilization campaign that is broadcast on weekly radio programs and through social media outlets. For the first time, Zimbabwean youth are discussing and debating issues related to their participation in elections. The campaign's popularity continues to expand, and the ZEC has been critical to its success. ZEC staff members regularly participate in the radio program and field live questions from listeners on the challenges they face in attempting to register. Similar programs use engaging events such as theater and music concerts as an opportunity to have well-known Zimbabweans disseminate information on elections and the importance of voting. Other voter outreach activities have been conducted through townhall style meetings, community dialogue, and community newsletters.

Given the history of violence associated with Zimbabwean elections, peace-building and reconciliation are critical, and faith-based organizations play a central role. As a complement to voter mobilization activities, the United States supports faith-based organizations' efforts to conduct large-scale peace rallies that feature gospel music and other performances. Messages calling for peaceful elections are delivered by representatives from across the political spectrum as well as religious leaders, and thousands of Zimbabweans turn out for each event.

The second pillar of USAID support focuses on observation of the election process in accordance with the principles of the Southern Africa Development Community (SADC)—the regional organization that has been monitoring implementation of the GPA. USAID and other donors are supporting domestic observation efforts. However, avenues to support international observation are more limited. Despite calls from the international community and Zimbabwean civil society for long-term international or regional observers to document the preelection environment, the current Electoral Law does not provide a mechanism for accrediting long-term observers—a critical gap. At this point in time, the USG is not funding regional or international observation delegations and it remains unclear whether the Government of Zimbabwe will accredit such observers in a timeframe allowing them to make an informed assessment of the overall electoral process. It is important to note even before elections take place that trust in the credibility of the election is not possible if long-term observers are not allowed.

The third pillar of our support is in the critical area of election administration. Efforts are underway to secure approval of a memorandum of understanding between the International Foundation for Electoral Systems (IFES) and the Government of Zimbabwe, which would enable USAID to provide support for the ZEC's priority actions. In the interim, USAID supports election administration strengthening and civil society efforts to provide evidence-based research and information on election-related best practices in the region. The goal is to provide this information to key stakeholders, including Parliamentarians and members of the ZEC, to ensure that Zimbabwe's legal and regulatory frameworks provide a foundation for transparent and credible electoral processes consistent with international norms and guidelines.

Supporting each of these three pillars is USAID's overarching assistance to Zimbabwe. By providing basic services for Zimbabwe's citizens, we not only meet immediate needs of citizens but also demonstrate that better governance can lead to better lives. The United States provides substantial support to combat the spread of HIV through the President's Emergency Plan for AIDS Relief (PEPFAR). Other efforts are increasing food security—now a critical issue for Zimbabwe—and working to improve Zimbabwe's business enabling environment to attract private sector investment, particularly in the once-thriving agricultural sector. USAID is also working with the Ministries of Finance and Economic Planning to strengthen human and institutional capacity for economic policy analysis, and to rebuild Zimbabwe's statistical foundations for economic analysis. These activities encourage the use of evidence-based economic policy research as a counterpoint to politically driven debate around economic policies. They also seek to broadly disseminate policy research and analysis to encourage public- private dialogue to improve Zimbabwe's economic policies and strengthen the policymaking process. In the short term, given the targeted harassment and intimidation of human rights defenders and democracy advocates in the lead up to the elections, the United States will continue to prioritize human rights and conflict mitigation and management activities.

We continue to believe that the Government of Zimbabwe can promote conditions for a credible electoral process in the preelection period, on election day, and in the tabulation of results, and USAID will continue to support its efforts. At the same time, we need to maintain our vigilance to ensure that barriers to participation—whether it is through intimidation, media restrictions, or denial of public assembly in the period running up to the election—do not undermine the credibility of those results.

Thank you, Mr. Chairman, Ranking Member Flake, and members of the subcommittee for the continued commitment you have shown to the Zimbabwean people and your support for real reform within the government. I welcome any questions you might have.

Senator COONS. Thank you to both our witnesses. We will now begin a round of questions, 7 minutes at a time, if we might.

First, if I might, Ambassador Yamamoto, you mentioned a recent development regarding the AU and observers. Just fill us in with a little more detail about what role the African Union is playing, or could play, and how essential SADC has been, and could be, to ensuring a free, fair, and effective election.

Ambassador YAMAMOTO. Thank you, Senator. Right now SADC has taken the lead in the recent meeting this past weekend in response to, I think, some of the comments made by Prime Minister Tsvangirai that the electoral process needs to be much more broad-based, the ability for the electoral commissions to register people properly and for it to hold elections in a very free and not rushed environment.

So the July 31 timeframe, the SADC has gone back and said this has to be done according to the electoral process. The issue is that the African Union, which is a very positive development, is going to be sending or has sent election observers into Zimbabwe.

What we are trying to do is—and we encourage not only the leadership that SADC has taken, South Africa, which we commend, but also the African Union under its new leadership, the Chairman Madam Zuma. But also we look to the United Nations also to take a leadership role. I think these groups and international groups together can make a difference in moving Zimbabwe toward making the right decisions and having free, fair, and open elections.

Senator COONS. Assistant Administrator Gast, you mentioned these three pillars: empowering participants, election observers, and election administration. Talk, if you would, in a little more detail about what the Zimbabwean Electoral Commission, the ZEC, needs to be able to effectively administer an election and what these regional best practices are that you are trying to help present information about and support ZEC in implementing?

Mr. GAST. Senator Coons, there has been a recent change in the leadership at the ZEC, the Zimbabwe Electoral Commission. Joyce Kazembe, who is coming from the Supreme Court, was recently placed in charge of the commission back in March, and I think by and large, talking with our Embassy, our Ambassador, our USAID mission, and our international observers. There has been a sincere outreach on her part and some of the other commissioners to engage with international partners in a dialogue.

So we are seeing that they are reaching out to us to talk about issues related to the electoral process. We also understand that, in spite of earlier efforts of the Ministry of Justice to prevent the UNDP from coming in and conducting an assessment mission and in the future providing support, she has approached both the Ministry of Finance and the Ministry of Justice in trying to get other international groups, some of which we work with, to come in and help establish the milestones and help come up with budget figures on how much it would cost to run the elections.

Another, I think, important twist is that she is actually effectively engaging with civil society groups, and she is beginning a process now, although it is not complete, but she is beginning a process by which she would be able to register and accredit local civil society organizations to observe the elections.

Senator COONS. Does the Zimbabwean Government have the resources to conduct—let us assume just for the moment that the constitutional court issues a later deadline—does the Zimbabwean Government have the resources and the technical expertise to conduct a free, fair, and open election?

Mr. GAST. We think not on both questions. But we are not certain that—well, one, no one has seen a specific budget on what it would cost to administer the elections. I think that is one of the reasons why the commissioner is reaching out for international support.

Second, the Minister of Finance, his observation, his assessment, is roughly it would cost $78 million to run the elections. That may be a bit low, just looking at other elections where you are running multiple levels of elections, parliamentarians, Presidential election, local elections. So we think that is a bit low.

The third thing related to that is that he has only made available $20 million of the so-called $78 million that is needed to conduct elections. Part of it is that the government runs on a cash-based basis, meaning what is in the coffers is what is allocated. So he has initially allocated $20 million to get the elections under way, but more money is needed, obviously, very soon if the elections are to take place at the end of July.

Senator COONS. Is it possible for there to be credible elections on this short of a timeline with that modest of a budget, with the restrictions on observers, and with the limitations on engagement?

Mr. GAST. International observers do not believe that it is likely that we will have credible elections if we were to proceed with the July 31date, looking at all the milestones necessary, to include a credible voter registration process as well as an opportunity to audit the voter registry.

Senator COONS. Ambassador Yamamoto, you state in your prepared testimony—you imply that the administration may be prepared to reconsider some of the sanctions structure or at the very least to expand trade and investment with Zimbabwe if they, in fact, have peaceful, credible, transparent elections. On the other hand, I will just assert that it is possible that there are alternative actions we might take if these elections fall significantly short of the SADC criteria. Speak to that a little bit more, if you would.

Ambassador YAMAMOTO. Sure. Nothing is off the table. We will look at every issue and every option that is before us. But right now we are so focused just on what SADC has done to try to move these elections to a much more free, fairer opportunities for all sides, but also to kind of continue the good things that are happening.

Just one point is, you know, Tendai Biti, the Finance Minister, has signed this IMF staff monitoring program, which is going to help the finance become much more open and transparent on the finances part. But what we do not want to see is where we have progress in one area, but not progress in the main area, which is going to be the electoral process, because that ultimately is going to define where Zimbabwe goes to the future. That I think, Senator—and we agree with you—nothing is off the table.

Senator COONS. Are you concerned that even if there are relatively peaceful elections, there may not be a smooth transition to an appropriately elected future government?

Ambassador YAMAMOTO. That is correct.

Senator COONS. With that, I will hand it over to Senator Flake.

Senator FLAKE. Thank you.

Ambassador Yamamoto, you mentioned that we ought to seek for more U.N. intervention or involvement. What organ of the United Nations? Is the Security Council likely to move on this or is this General Assembly resolutions or what exactly are we looking for there? What would be useful?

Ambassador YAMAMOTO. I think right now that is an issue to be answered by the organizations that are dealing with Zimbabwe itself. Right now SADC has taken the lead, not only through the roadmap for the elections, but also the global political agreement that became really the hallmark, the framework, of where we are headed toward in Zimbabwe.

The input by the African Union recently with the electoral observers, that is important. But I think, in consultations between SADC, the African Union, and the United Nations to look at where each institution, organization, can play a role in moving Zimbabwe forward, I think it has to be a discussion with them.

Senator FLAKE. Mr. Gast, what has been the impact of the sanctions that we have imposed, the travel and other targeted sanctions on leaders? And what leverage do we have going forward in terms of their reaction? Do you see any movement based on these sanctions or not?

Mr. GAST. I will let my colleague talk specifically about the sanctions, but certainly because there are sanctions we are very careful about whom we work with in the country. So some of our economic programs, which really are a way of supporting small farmholders who did not have access to credit, and looking at linking them to buyers, we go through a very specific vetting process to make sure that anyone who is on any of the sanctions lists does not benefit from our assistance.

Senator FLAKE. Before we go back to answer that question, the new constitution, how does it address the land reform issue?

Mr. GAST. It does not address the land reform issue, and that is one of the problems, is that there is no secure land tenure in the country. As we were discussing in the back room, we see that there are two major—certainly one that is on the books now, the absence of land tenure, which means that no one can use the land as collateral for getting lending, and so there is no financing or no lending in the ag sector.

The second issue is indigenization, and they are looking at putting forward a more aggressive bill to support indigenization, which would require all international companies to divest themselves of ownership so that there is a minimum of 51 percent Zimbabwean ownership. So we feel that those are going to be two major—those are major impediments to investment going into Zimbabwe.

Senator FLAKE. With regard to sanctions, what has been the impact and what leverage do we have moving forward?

Ambassador YAMAMOTO. I think on the sanctions, of course, it is on 113 individuals and entities. They remain really the framework which we are using to work with the Zimbabwe Government to do the right things. I think the sanctions as they stand now is on assets and of course travel.

We are constantly reviewing and looking at how we can beef up, strengthen those sanctions. But I think for the time being the sanctions we have in place seem to be our policy for the time being, and it is always under constant review.

One thing on the land reform is, we are also looking at that very, very carefully, because on the land reform, if we cannot have the Zimbabwean Government move forward on a rationalization of land, but more important is the transference of land with titles, that I think is going to be bad for not only the economy, but I think on the overall stability of the country.

Senator FLAKE. With regard to the electoral process, Mr. Gast, you mentioned that the preelection requirements have not—there is insufficient time to get those in place. What amount of time is needed in your estimation to have these in place?

Mr. GAST. There are a number of laws and the constitution have very strict timelines. So there is some conflict among them. Parliament goes out of session at the end of June and there is a 4-month gap by which elections have to be held. So if you extend that out, elections have to be held no later than some time in October.

The other requirements are the fact that there has to be a 30-day voter registration process and then another 30 days to review and audit the rolls, as well as time for the political parties to nominate candidates. Again, we are dealing with multiple levels of elections, so parliamentary as well as local elections. And then for those candidates to be announced, as well as the campaigning period.

So, using that as a timeline, others in the MDC and other observers have said that potentially one could meet—they could meet the milestones if elections were pushed back about 30 days toward the end of August.

Senator FLAKE. With regard to the economy, you mentioned 5 percent growth or some estimates as high as 7. Is this artificial? Can this be maintained, assuming we have some version of the status quo after the election? Do you believe that the economic growth that has occurred over the past year or so will continue, Ambassador?

Ambassador YAMAMOTO. I think those will be held in jeopardy if the elections are not free, fair, open, because it would send a message to investors that the government has reneged on its commitment toward those electoral processes. The end result is if you do not have confidence in that government the investments will start to dry up. So that is why we said that the government and the people of Zimbabwe are really at a crossroads with these elections.

Senator FLAKE. In recent years the government has collateralized a lot of the industry and minerals there. To what extent have they gone? I think the airport near Victoria Falls, commercial activity has been mortgaged, if you will. Some of the mineral rights. What else has the government done in order to meet short-term cash flow needs?

Ambassador YAMAMOTO. We would have to get back to you on the specificity. Just on some of its intake and revenues, we are seeing that they have not capitalized on a lot of the resources that they have exported and that they have not taken full advantage. Of course, that becomes mainly due because of lack of transparency.

One of the issues that we support with the IMF on the staff monitoring program is that it gives greater transparency to financial resources and intake.

But we will get back to you on more information.

[EDITOR'S NOTE.—A response to the above question was not supplied by the time this hearing went to press.]

Senator FLAKE. Thank you, Mr. Chairman.

Senator COONS. Thank you, Senator Flake.

Ambassador, your written testimony raises concern about the diversion of diamond revenues to the security sector that is directly or indirectly being used in suppressing civil liberties. What is the United States doing to address those concerns and have concerns like this been addressed effectively through the Kimberley Process or is the Kimberley Process not either relevant or effective, moving forward, to ensuring that natural resources revenues are taken care of responsibly and appropriately in Zimbabwe?

Ambassador YAMAMOTO. As you know, Senator—thank you, Senator. For 1 year we were the chair for the Kimberley Process and we made a great effort to look at rationalizing how the Marange mines are operated, how free and fair and open it is in its operations, and that money from the diamonds are not diverted.

As you know, from the resources and the amount of diamonds that Zimbabwe has they can earn probably as much as $600 million a year or more. Right now the estimate is about $47 million. So the question comes in is what happened? Where is that? Where is the money? Are they not efficient in how they sell those diamonds, or is it being diverted toward other means that are illicit or not in keeping with support of the general public? Those are questions that we constantly ask.

We do not have the complete answers, but we only have concerns that those moneys are not being used for the support of the people of Zimbabwe.

Senator COONS. So do you think the Kimberley Process continues to be relevant to this conversation?

Ambassador YAMAMOTO. Yes.

Senator COONS. And what more can we or should we do moving forward?

Ambassador YAMAMOTO. I think the Kimberley Process, what we try to do is make it a much more rational and decisive institution and organization. I think its establishment has been effective in trying to control the flow of diamonds and it remains relevant in how we manage the diamond markets. I think it also holds Zimbabwe and other countries in many ways accountable to what they need to be doing on the diamonds.

But let me just also add on the sanctions, on the 113 individuals and 7 entities. What it does do, too, is that it limits the ability of the mining sector to distribute diamonds or conflict minerals to the United States and to other countries.

Senator COONS. The Vice Premier of China visited Zimbabwe last month and I have raised in previous hearings concerns about ways in which China's expanding economic role in the continent may provide a counterweight to our values agenda around democracy, human rights, open media, and so forth. Do expanding Chinese interests in Zimbabwe lessen incentives for the government to improve respect for human rights, or is China simply positioning itself to play a stronger role in the economy in a way that does not influence the elections or the outcome? Any input for me, Assistant Administrator Gast or Ambassador Yamamoto, on the role China is playing?

Mr. GAST. China, obviously, has a noninterference approach, which means that they do not engage the government on reforms. As we have always said, U.S. business is great for the continent in so many ways because it also brings good governance principles. We do not see that when we see Chinese investment.

The deals generally are shrouded in secrecy. There is no transparency and it actually helps to further, if you will, corruption or corrupt practices.

Ambassador YAMAMOTO. If I can add one point to that.

Senator COONS. Please, Ambassador.

Ambassador YAMAMOTO. We are headed into our seventh bilateral discussions with the Chinese that we started several years ago. These are some of the issues that we have raised with the Chinese directly, that if they are going to use the resources—and right now they are at $150 billion and that is mainly raw materials and resources from Africa—if they are going to be focused on that, then they have to look at what is good for, or will help benefit, the people in Africa and make sure that all these resources are accountable and accounted for.

So those are some of the things that we are looking at. Yes, there are a lot of areas that we have deep concerns, but I think through these negotiations and meetings annually that we are addressing these, and it is going to be very tough negotiations and talks.

Senator COONS. Well, if Zimbabwe were to change and if we were to see a changed timeline, with free and fair and open elections, an orderly election, and a peaceful transition to a new government, what might we be able to do in response? What sort of expanded programs or activities might USAID take that would significantly increase economic opportunity and improve the lot of the average Zimbabwean?

Mr. GAST. Obviously, we have been consulting with like-minded donors and also some of the major financial institutions—African Development Bank and World Bank. Obviously, institution-building would be needed, putting in good systems of accountable governance, to include economic governance.

But one area that could make a big difference in Zimbabwe is in the agricultural sector, doing more in supporting small landholders, getting people employed in the ag sector, and starting with that. The industries that have languished over the years will take years and years of investment before they come back in line, but to make an immediate impact we feel that on the economic side the focus should be on agriculture and linking small farmholders, landholders, to larger markets and also buyers in the region.

Senator COONS. These are areas where USAID and other elements of the U.S. Government have successfully led significant initiatives and investment and have made real progress in other countries in the region?

Mr. GAST. In other countries, and we are also doing very similar things with some of the small landholders in Zimbabwe. So we are working with approximately 90,000 landholders, families that own land, and helping provide them with technical assistance in good farming techniques, access to inputs, and also, more importantly, access to credit.

Senator COONS. Last question, if I might, for both of you. What are the specific benchmarks or the conditions that would have to be met to justify increasing engagement with, or support for, the Zimbabwean Government going forward?

Mr. GAST. Our Ambassador has publicly stated in Zimbabwe that credible, peaceful elections is absolutely a must before we can talk about further engagement and deepening engagement with the Government of Zimbabwe.

Ambassador YAMAMOTO. And based on that framework, we can work on the other areas, such as media freedoms, the agriculture, the economy, and the finance.

Then just to add to what my colleague has said, in striking terms Zimbabwe should be the breadbasket for southern Africa. It should be. It is importing food. We are providing humanitarian assistance for—in the nineties—7 million people. It is now down to 1.6 million. But that should not be the case. This is a rich, very rich country. It should be the leading light for southern Africa. As the regional leaders have said, this is as much a problem for these countries as it is for Zimbabwe and the people of Zimbabwe.

Senator COONS. So to summarize, let me just make sure I hear you right. Credible, free, fair elections are the beginning, beyond which there are other critical benchmarks, including a transition to a new government and progress on human rights, media freedoms, and so forth.

Thank you very much.

Senator Flake.

Senator FLAKE. Well, that was my question, Is what would constitute progress enough—sufficient for us to normalize relations, to remove the sanctions?

Let me just say, I met with MDC officials a couple years ago. They were calling for relaxing some of these sanctions. Obviously, Andrew Young and others who have gone there have called for that as well. To what extent is the opposition, the MDC and others, publicly still calling for normalization or at least some kind of lessening or weakening of these sanctions? And is that their true feeling or is that a public posture that they feel differently otherwise? What is your assessment there?

Ambassador YAMAMOTO. That is a very difficult question to answer in a public forum. The issue for the sanctions is, yes, regional leaders have approached us and said that if sanctions were lifted Zimbabwe could have a freer access toward developing their economy and reaching out to its people. Our position has been that the sanctions are there because the government has not reached out to its people, because it has not done the right things in various areas. So those sanctions remain.

As we told the MDC people and the others, the MDC, that these sanctions are in their interests as well, and they understand that. And ZANU–PF also understands why those sanctions are in place and they are going to remain so until there is changes.

Senator FLAKE. What motivated our recent decision to waive the sanctions with regard to the African Development Bank?

Ambassador YAMAMOTO. You mean the Agriculture and the Infrastructure Development Banks? Those were our normal review of sanctions. So the eight individuals, eight individuals and entity that we looked at, we looked at whether or not they were making progress toward being much more open and transparent in their processes and their restrictions.

Anyway, so in that regards we had determined through the sanctions review process that they were meeting some of those trend-lines and so therefore we lifted just part of the sanctions.

Senator FLAKE. Mr. Gast, do you think that State and the impact at AID—do we have the flexibility that we need, the administration, with regard to these sanctions to help try to prompt change or the kind of behavior that we want?

Mr. GAST. At this point we do, and we have also built in flexibility into our existing program and our strategy to allow us to move into areas where there are openings, provided that there is good progress with regard to the elections and human rights.

Senator FLAKE. All right. Thank you, Mr. Chairman.

Senator COONS. I would like to thank our first panel. Thank you very much, Ambassador Yamamoto. Thank you, Assistant Administrator Gast, both for your leadership, for your insights, and for your important testimony today.

I would now like to turn to our second panel, and we will wait for a moment for the transition from the first to the second panel. Thank you so much for your testimony.

[Pause.]

Senator COONS. I would now like to turn to our second panel, starting with Mr. Mahvinga, followed by Mr. Schneider and finally Mr. Moss. Gentlemen, thank you so much for being with us today. I have given a brief overview of your current positions and responsibilities in my introduction and I would now like to invite Mr. Mahvinga to offer your opening statement.

STATEMENT OF DEWA MAHVINGA, SENIOR RESEARCHER, HUMAN RIGHTS WATCH, WASHINGTON, DC

Mr. MAHVINGA. Thank you, Chairman Coons, Ranking Member Flake, and other members of the committee, for providing Human Rights Watch with the opportunity to testify on this hearing on Zimbabwe. I would like to request that my statement be submitted for the record.

Senator COONS. Without objection.

Mr. MAHVINGA. My name is Dewa Mahvinga. I am a senior researcher with the Africa Division of Human Rights Watch, where I lead our work on Zimbabwe. I frequently travel to Zimbabwe and last month I met the leaders of the main political parties, media, key civil society groups, church leaders, and business people to assess the human rights conditions ahead of the coming elections. I also maintain daily contact with local activists, who keep me informed of the situation in Zimbabwe.

Mr. Chairman, my testimony will first lay out the human rights trends in Zimbabwe and then highlight key recommendations for the U.S. Government for action to promote a rights-respecting environment leading to credible, transparent, peaceful elections and political stability thereafter.

Many people in Zimbabwe have expectations that the elections will usher in a democratically elected government with interest in addressing the country's long-standing and serious human rights issues. But as things stand, there is a slim chance that Zimbabwe will have free, fair, and credible elections, particularly given the shortcomings of security sector reforms and reforms in other sectors.

On June 13, President Robert Mugabe used a Presidential decree to set July 31 as the election date for harmonized elections. It is critically important that these elections should be held under conditions where Zimbabweans can freely vote for leadership of their choice. As you may know, on June 15 the leaders of the Southern African Development Community, SADC, urged President Mugabe to approach Zimbabwe's constitutional court to seek extension or delays to elections to allow for much-needed electoral reforms before elections. The Government of Zimbabwe has said it does not have funds for elections.

Mr. Chairman, during my visit to Zimbabwe last month people told me of their great fear of the coming elections, that they might just be another cycle of violence because little has changed on the ground. They told me of their despair when they see people responsible for the 2008 violence working free because the so-called unity government has failed to hold them accountable. Instead of focusing on pulling themselves out of this poverty and rebuilding their lives, they are bracing themselves for further violence and chaos.

I had the opportunity to interview the home affairs minister, Theresa Mekone of the MDC, who is responsible for the voters roll, about the ongoing process of updating the voters roll. She told me that when she checked her own name was missing from the roll. After complaining about it in Cabinet, she later checked again and found that her name had been removed from the roll. When then she checked for the second time, it had been placed there, but spelled incorrectly. The voter registration process and the voters roll updating process is marred with errors, to what extent deliberate unclear.

A key benchmark for the U.S. Government here as it reconsiders its policy toward Zimbabwe should be the assessment of whether or not the country is prepared and has held peaceful, transparent, fair, and free elections, and also that the government-elect has been able to assume power. Simply basing the U.S. policy on the holding of a peaceful referendum on the constitution, which took place in March, is not enough.

On the human rights landscape, Mr. Chairman, there have been some reforms. We now have a new constitution that has been agreed to last month. It is a significant reform, but alone it is not sufficient because of challenges relating to the security sector.

A number of new national commissions have been established, including the Zimbabwe Electoral Commission, the Zimbabwe Media Commission, the Anti-Corruption Commission, and the Zimbabwe Human Rights Commission. The Zimbabwe Human Rights Commission is not functional because of lack of resources, so it has no capacity the influence positively the human rights environment as we go into elections.

The Zimbabwe Media Commission has licensed new newspapers, but there is limited opening of the free air waves in terms of electronic media in terms of the radio and television.

A key challenge for Zimbabwe as we go into elections which is really crucial to be addressed is the role that Zimbabwe state security forces would play, particularly the defense forces, the police, and the Central Intelligence Organization.

I turn now to recommendations for the U.S. Government that we request: Close collaboration with the Southern African Development Community, SADC, for the United States in terms of pushing for free and fair elections. We urge the U.S. Government to ensure that before there is consideration for a shift in policy or a review of sanctions this should be based on whether or not the country has had peaceful elections and whether the government-elect has assumed power.

We also urge the Obama administration to work closely with SADC to ensure strict political neutrality on the part of the security forces and to ensure that they refrain from partisan statements supporting one political party over the other.

We also urge for urgent reforms to the highly partisan state-controlled print and electronic media.

We also urge that there be immediate deployment of domestic and SADC-led international election observers in sufficient numbers to allow for effective monitoring of the situation and to promote credible, free, and fair elections in line with the SADC standards.

We also urge that the Zimbabwe Government should immediately repeal all repressive legislation, including the Access to Information and Protection of Privacy Act, the Public Order and Security Act, the Criminal Procedures and Evidence Act, which are hindering freedom of expression for the people of Zimbabwe as they go into elections.

We urge the U.S. Government to provide financial and technical support for a government that comes into power through credible, free, and fair elections in a manner that would strengthen democratic state institutions in the areas of promoting the rule of law, democracy, good governance, and human rights.

Mr. Chairman, my sincere thanks again for this opportunity to address this committee. I am happy to respond to questions from you or from your colleagues. Thank you.

[The prepared statement of Mr. Mahvinga follows:]

PREPARED STATEMENT OF DEWA MAVHINGA

INTRODUCTION

Thank you, Chairman Coons, Ranking Member Flake, and other members of the committee for providing Human Rights Watch the opportunity to testify at this hearing on Zimbabwe. I would like to request that my statement in its entirety be submitted for the record.

My name is Dewa Mavhinga. I am a senior researcher with the Africa Division of Human Rights Watch where I lead our work on Zimbabwe. I frequently travel to Zimbabwe and last month met with leaders of the main political parties, private media, and key civil society groups to assess human rights conditions ahead of the coming elections. I maintain daily contact with local activists, civil society and church leaders, and business people from Zimbabwe who keep me up to date regarding the situation there.

Mr. Chairman, my testimony will first lay out the human rights situation in Zimbabwe and then highlight key recommendations to the U.S. Government for action to promote a rights-respecting environment leading to credible, transparent, and peaceful elections and political stability thereafter. Many people in Zimbabwe have expectations that the elections will usher in a democratically elected government with interest in addressing the country's longstanding and serious human rights issues. But as things stand currently, the chances of having free, fair, and credible elections are slim, particularly given the shortcomings of security sector reforms and reforms in other sectors.

On June 13, President Robert Mugabe used a Presidential decree to set July 31, 2013, as the date for national "harmonized" elections, that is, parliamentary, Presidential and local government elections. These are critically important elections that should be held under conditions in which Zimbabweans are able to freely vote for leadership of their choice. As you may know, on June 15, leaders of the Southern African Development Community (SADC) urged Mugabe to approach Zimbabwe's Constitutional Court to seek a 2-week delay to elections to allow for much-needed electoral reforms before elections. The Government of Zimbabwe has said it does not have funds for elections.

Mr. Chairman, during my visit to Zimbabwe last month, people told me of their great fear that the coming elections might just be another cycle of political violence because little had changed on the ground to build their confidence that they can vote freely. They told me of their despair when they see the people responsible for the 2008 violence, whom the unity government failed to hold accountable, walking free. Instead of focusing on pulling themselves out of poverty and on rebuilding lives shattered by the 2008 political violence, they were bracing themselves for further violence and chaos.

I had opportunity to interview Zimbabwe's home affairs minister, Theresa Makone of MDC, responsible for the voters roll, about the ongoing process of updating the voters roll. Despite having voted in 2008, when she checked on the voters roll she found her own name was missing. After complaining about it in the Cabinet, she later checked again and found her name on the roll, but spelled incorrectly. The voter registration and voters roll updating process is marred with errors—to what extent deliberate is unclear.

A key benchmark for the U.S. Government here, as it reconsiders its policy toward Zimbabwe should be the assessment of whether the country has not only managed to have peaceful, transparent, free and fair elections, but also that the government-elect has been able to assume power. Simply basing the U.S. policy on the March 16 constitutional referendum is insufficient all three main political parties campaigned for the adoption of the new constitution—and it is only one successful stop along a long road of change.

Instead, positive engagements with Mugabe and his Zimbabwe African National Union-Patriotic Front (ZANU–PF) party should be conditioned on tangible progress in improving respect for human rights and the rule of law in Zimbabwe. Mugabe's recent calls for peace are not enough; there is need for matching action to demonstrate a commitment to nonviolence and to peaceful elections.

I. THE HUMAN RIGHTS LANDSCAPE

The human rights landscape in Zimbabwe is characterized by a mixture of modest reforms in the context of a number of necessary reforms that remain outstanding if genuine change is to occur.

A. "Unity Government" Reforms

In September 2008 President Mugabe's ZANU–PF and the two factions of the Movement for Democratic Change (MDC) party, led by Morgan Tsvangirai and Arthur Mutambara, agreed to a Global Political Agreement (GPA) to form a power-sharing government, formed officially in February 2009. The main purpose of the so-called unity government was to establish institutional and legal reforms to create a conducive environment for the holding of free and fair elections.

The unity government, however, left Mugabe and ZANU–PF—because of their control of key government ministries including defense, state security, and justice—with significantly greater power than the MDC, which has been used to frustrate or stop crucial reforms. Over 4 years since the GPA was signed, the unity government has made some progress only in implementing those parts of the agreement that do not address political violence or create conditions for credible elections.

Establishment of a New Constitution

Perhaps the most significant reform is the establishment of the new constitution, signed into law by President Mugabe on May 22, 2013, following a March 16 referendum and approval by the Zimbabwe Parliament. The new constitution, which replaces the 1979 Lancaster House Constitution, may prove beneficial to the electoral process as it prohibits any changes to the electoral law once elections have been called. It has a more expansive bill of rights, and it restores citizenship and voting rights to those born in Zimbabwe to a parent or parents with citizenship of another SADC country but resident in Zimbabwe.

While very important, the new constitution is only one of the reforms required for an environment conducive for credible elections. A number of laws, including the electoral laws, require amendment to be brought in line with the provisions of the new constitution. For the new constitution to benefit all Zimbabweans government leaders and state institutions must respect the constitution and fulfill its provisions. Failure to act in accordance with constitutional provisions has been a major challenge contributing to a poor human rights environment in the country.

Establishment of National Commissions

The unity government established four new national commissions—the Zimbabwe Electoral Commission (ZEC), the reconstituted Zimbabwe Media Commission, the Anti-Corruption Commission, and the Zimbabwe Human Rights Commission (ZHRC).

The Zimbabwe Electoral Commission's Secretariat staff is dominated by partisan state intelligence and military officials. Electoral reforms are essential if the Zimbabwe Electoral Commission is to be independent and professional. Further, the voters roll needs to be updated and to be placed under ZEC's exclusive control.

The potential impact of the Zimbabwe Human Rights Commission on the human rights environment, particularly curtailing impunity for serious abuses, is undermined by the commission's limited mandate and jurisdiction—it is insufficiently retroactive as it can only investigate and address human rights abuses committed since February 13, 2009, when the unity government was formed. Notably, it is not empowered to address the widespread electoral violence of 2008. Also problematic is that the ZHRC is not fully operational to address human rights complaints or carry out its core mandate because of lack of resources to recruit technical staff and procure essential office equipment.

The Zimbabwe Media Commission has licensed new newspapers, including the once banned Daily News, that are now operating in the country, but the media remain under the shadow of repressive legislation that severely restricts rights to freedom of expression and association. This includes broad sections of the Criminal Law (Codification and Reform) Act on criminal defamation or publicly making statements that may cause feelings of hostility toward or cause hatred, ridicule, or contempt of the President—whether in person or in respect of the Office of President.

The ZANU–PF minister for media, information, and publicity unilaterally and controversially constituted the Broadcasting Authority of Zimbabwe (BAZ), which has since issued two private commercial radio licenses as part of the commitment to free up the airwaves. The first commercial radio station, Star FM, is owned by Zimpapers—a state-owned company that publishes all state-owned newspapers, including the ZANU–PF-aligned Herald daily newspaper. The only other private commercial radio license was awarded to AB Communications to run ZiFM Radio.

There is concern that the two radio stations will be highly partisan reflecting their close links to Mugabe and ZANU–PF. For instance, Supa Mandiwanzira, the founder and chief executive officer at ZiFM Radio, is the ZANU–PF treasurer for Manicaland province.

Despite the provision in the roadmap to elections that new, independent boards for the Mass Media Trust and the Zimbabwe Broadcasting Corporation should be appointed to make state-owned broadcasting and print media politically neutral, this has not happened. There have been limited media reforms to ensure that the highly partisan state-controlled print and electronic media become genuinely public, to guarantee equal and fair coverage to all political parties.

B. No Meaningful Security Sector, Legal & Institutional Reforms

The Zimbabwe unity government's failure to introduce and implement far-reaching reforms in the security sector and in other sectors has a huge bearing on the human rights situation in the country especially around elections.

Highly Partisan and Politicized Security Forces

Crucial for the elections—and the government that comes to power—will be the role played by Zimbabwe's state security forces, particularly the Defense Forces, the police, and the Central Intelligence Organization (CIO). The security forces have a long history of partisanship on behalf of President Mugabe and ZANU–PF. Since independence in 1980, the army, police, and CIO have operated within a system that has allowed elements within their ranks to arbitrarily arrest, torture, and kill perceived opponents with impunity.

Zimbabwe's security forces, notably the military, have for several years interfered in the nation's political and electoral affairs in ways that have adversely affected the ability of citizens to vote freely. This was particularly evident during the 2008 elections, in which the army played a major role in the widespread and systematic abuses that led to the killing of at least to 200 people, the beating and torture of 5,000 more, and the displacement of about 36,000 others. Since then the leadership of the military, police and CIO, all appointed by Mugabe, remain unchanged, as have their clear, public and vocal support for Mugabe and ZANU–PF.

The partisanship of the security forces' leadership has translated into abuses by these forces against MDC members and supporters, and civil society organizations. Beyond the open endorsement of ZANU–PF, the security forces have been deployed across the country where they have intimidated, beaten, and committed other abuses against Zimbabweans perceived to be supporting the MDC or critical of the ZANU–PF officials in government.

Although Zimbabwe's various laws, as well as the new constitution, require neutrality and impartiality from the security forces, no effort has been made to enforce them. No members of the security forces are known to have been disciplined or prosecuted for acting in a partisan manner in support of ZANU–PF or committing criminal offenses against the MDC and its supporters. Concerns about the role of the security forces extend not only to situation prior to election day and the voting itself, but to the critical post-election period.

There is an urgent need, ahead of the elections, to ensure that the new constitutional provisions prohibiting members of the security services from acting in a partisan manner and from being active members or office-bearers of any political party or organization are enforced to ensure strict political neutrality. Should the security forces fail to adopt a professional, independent and nonpartisan role during elections, other recent reforms may be insufficient to deliver the elections needed to put Zimbabwe on a democratic and rights-respecting track.

Restrictions on Rights to Freedom of Expression, Association, and Assembly

The unity government has failed to make any changes to repressive laws such as the Access to Information and Protection of Privacy Act (AIPPA), the Public Order and Security Act (POSA), and the Criminal Law (Codification and Reform) Act. These laws have been used to severely curtail basic rights through vague defamation clauses and draconian penalties. Provisions dealing with criminal defamation and undermining the authority of or insulting the president have been routinely used against journalists and political activists.

Partisan policing and prosecution has worsened the impact of the repressive provisions in POSA and AIPPA laws. Often the police have deliberately misinterpreted provisions of POSA to ban lawful public meetings and gatherings, including religious meetings that are exempt from police permission where the requirement is only for police to be notified. Failure to repeal or significantly revise these laws and to develop mechanisms to address the partisan conduct of the police leaves little chance of a full enjoyment of the rights to freedom of association and assembly in the runup to and during the coming elections.

The Criminal Procedure and Evidence Act in section 121 effectively permits prosecutors to overturn judicial rulings granting bail and extend detention time by 7 days. It has frequently been used by prosecutors targeting political and civil society activists who work with local human rights organizations.

Police Crackdown on Civil Society

Since December 2012, the ZANU–PF-controlled police have carried out a campaign of politically motivated abuses against civil society activists and organizations, including the harassment and 8-day detention of human rights lawyer, Beatrice Mtetwa, despite a High Court order for her release. The judge who issued the court order for her release was later charged with misconduct by the Supreme Court's Chief Justice. At time of writing the judge's misconduct case was pending consideration by President Mugabe.

On March 8, 2013, in Harare, police charged Jestina Mukoko, director of the Zimbabwe Peace Project, with leading an unregistered organization under the Private Voluntary Organization (PVO) Act, and with smuggling radios and mobile phones into the country in violation of the Broadcasting Services Act and the Customs and Excise Act. The charges under the PVO Act violate the right to freedom of association, while the other charges appear to be a politically motivated attempt to curtail the group's human rights work.

On February 13 and 14, police in Harare and Bulawayo forcibly disrupted the annual Valentine's Day ''love'' protests by about 190 members of Women of Zimbabwe Arise (WOZA). The police arbitrarily arrested, detained and in some cases beat with batons protesters, including the WOZA national coordinator, Jenni Williams. The protesters were released without charge following the intervention of lawyers.

On February 11, in what appears to have been coordinated action, police raided the offices of the National Association of NGOs (NANGO) and Community Tolerance Reconciliation and Development (COTRAD) in Masvingo and the Zimbabwe Peace Project (ZPP) offices in Harare.

On March 8, the ZANU–PF-controlled Zimbabwe Electoral Commission announced that any civil society organization under police investigation would be barred from monitoring the constitutional referendum and elections. This directive directly affected the main civil society organizations operating in the country, including ZPP, Zimbabwe Human Rights Association (ZimRights), Zimbabwe Election Support Network, and Crisis in Zimbabwe Coalition.

The recent police actions against civil society groups appear to have had the approval of the highest levels of the police. At the Senior Police Officers' Conference in November 2012, attended by country's top police officers, an official statement was approved noting "with concern the negative influence and subversive activities" of nongovernmental and civil society organizations in the coming referendum and elections.

A similar resolution was approved at the December 2012 ZANU–PF annual conference, which was attended by all security chiefs. ZANU–PF resolved to "instruct the party to ensure that government enforces the de-registration of errant [organizations] deviating from their mandate."

Soon after these statements were approved, the police began a sustained and systematic campaign of harassment and intimidation of civil society organizations. On December 13, police raided the offices of ZimRights and arrested four people, including one of the organization's staff. A month later, on January 14, police arrested the ZimRights national director, Okay Machisa, ostensibly in his capacity as director of the organization, on charges relating to a voter registration campaign. Machisa spent over 2 weeks in detention before being released on bail.

On January 18, the ZANU–PF minister for youth and indigenization, Saviour Kasukuwere, formally approved regulations requiring all youth organizations to be registered with the Zimbabwe Youth Council or to be banned. Under these regulations, no youth organization may receive funding without authorization from the youth council and all members or affiliates of registered youth organizations are required to pay exorbitant annual levies to the youth council. These regulations may cripple the operations of youth organizations throughout the country.

The systematic police campaign against civil society organizations may be a deliberate attempt to disrupt the operations of civil society organizations and stop them from monitoring the human rights environment ahead of the elections.

II. KEY RECOMMENDATIONS TO THE US GOVERNMENT

The U.S. Government has a strong interest in promoting respect for the rule of law, good governance, and human rights. In southern Africa, the United States can safeguard and promote these interests by supporting the people of Zimbabwe at this time by helping to minimize the risk of the country sliding back to political chaos and widespread rights violations.

As the United States considers the best way to assist the Zimbabwean people to resolve their human rights and governance crisis, we urge Congress to consider the following measures.

(1) Ensure that any shift in U.S. policy toward Zimbabwe, including a review of sanctions, is based on an assessment of whether the country has managed to have peaceful, transparent, free and fair elections and whether the government-elect can assume power.

(2) Call on the Obama administration to work closely with the Southern African Development Community (SADC) to press Zimbabwe's political leaders to urgently take steps to:

- Ensure the political neutrality of the security forces, namely by investigating and prosecuting alleged abuses by security force personnel, publicly directing the leadership of the security forces to carry out their responsibilities in a professional and impartial manner, and appropriately punishing or prosecuting those who fail to do so;
- Press for urgent reforms to the highly partisan state-controlled print and electronic media to ensure that they become genuinely public, to guarantee equal and fair coverage to all political parties;
- Provide for the immediate deployment, and in sufficient numbers, of both domestic and SADC-led international election observers to Zimbabwe and maintain such monitors for a sufficient period after elections to deter violence and intimidation and to promote credible, free and fair elections that comply with the SADC Principles and Guidelines Governing Democratic Elections;

- Ensure implementation of all electoral reforms envisaged in the new constitution including the updating and cleaning up the country's outdated voters' roll, which has a significant number of "ghost" voters; and
- Ensure that the Zimbabwe Government repeals or amends all repressive legislation such as the repressive sections of the Criminal Law (Codification and Reform) Act, the Public Order and Security Act, the Access to Information and Protection of Privacy Act and section 121 of the Criminal Procedure and Evidence Act.

(3) Provide financial and technical support for a government that comes to power through credible, free, and fair elections in a manner that would strengthen democratic state institutions and promote the rule of law, democracy, good governance, and human rights.

Mr. Chairman, my sincere thanks once again for the opportunity to address this committee. I am happy to respond to any questions you or your colleagues may have.

Senator COONS. Thank you, Mr. Mahvinga.
Mr. Schneider.

STATEMENT OF MARK SCHNEIDER, SENIOR VICE PRESIDENT, INTERNATIONAL CRISIS GROUP, WASHINGTON, DC

Mr. SCHNEIDER. Mr. Chairman, let me express my appreciation to you and to Senator Flake and members of the Senate Foreign Relations Subcommittee on Africa for the opportunity to testify this morning and for focusing attention on what we do see as a looming electoral crisis in Zimbabwe.

Crisis Group, as you know, is independent, nonpartisan, and nongovernmental. We try and provide field-based analysis of the drivers of conflict and offer some policy prescriptions to try and prevent deadly violence or to bring it to an end where it exists.

We have reported on Zimbabwe's dismal state of governance, deterioration of human rights, and worsening economic conditions for more than a decade. In March 2008 our preelectoral report was entitled "Prospects from a Flawed Election." Unless urgent actions are taken over the next several weeks, we fear Zimbabwe is facing déjà vu and essentially return to the same potential chaos that we saw in 2008.

Our May report, which I believe the committee has, cited the absence of a level playing field. Recent actions have tilted the playing surface even more sharply. Last Thursday, for the first time since the coalition government of ZANU–PF and the two MDC factions was formed, President Robert Mugabe issued his first Presidential decree under emergency power, setting the election date for 31 July. He issued a second decree which short-circuited the democratic process, overrode constitutional electoral timelines. It shortened voter registration. It shortened candidate registration, and it shortened periods for the campaign itself, and in so doing immediately drew challenges from the MDC and civil society as unfair and unconstitutional.

This weekend, the SADC heads of state met as the oversight and monitoring authority on compliance with the Global Political Agreement and received South African President Jacob Zuma's report on Zimbabwe. He essentially cited some of those same concerns. He noted, in words that we would echo, that the GPA commitment was that, "elections shall be held under conditions where all parties shall participate freely, on equal footing, in an environment free of intimidation and violence, and that this is necessary to bring into being the next government, which shall enjoy undisputed credibility.''

Essentially, without those reforms and without that kind of credible election, Zimbabwe is going to find itself again essentially as an outcast. It should be noted that his report, which I assume the committee has, the recommendations were endorsed by the SADC heads of state in that communique, and thus far they noted that the failure—they have seen the failure to see the adoption of reforms on media, political participation, security, electoral procedures, and they noted that the 31 July date, ''is fraught with legal contestation, political dispute, and heightened tensions.''

They specifically urged all of the parties in Zimbabwe to seek more time. Some have interpreted that as 2 weeks. That is not what the communique said. That is not what President Zuma's report said. It said seek more time, essentially to ensure that the opportunity for a fair and free election is there.

The reason why is that 6 weeks prior now to July 31, there is no agreed and final registration rolls, there is no electoral law approved by the Parliament, no candidates formally nominated or approved by the nomination court, not only for President, but for 358 parliamentary seats and local and urban and rural councils as well. There is little time for ballots to be printed, less time for them to be distributed to basically 9,500 polling stations, and no time for the 30-day campaign set out in the constitution after the candidates are approved. There is no testing of electronic tabulation processes, no agreement yet for who the domestic electoral monitors can be, nor authorization for international electoral monitoring, and no transparent indication of how the election will be funded, which the committee has already raised in the previous testimony.

Our single greatest worry, however, is the conduct of Zimbabwe's security forces leading up to elections, the day of elections, and the post-election period. We have urged, obviously, an end to state-sponsored violence, for security reform, protection of civil society and political party activists as necessary to end the politics of fear in Zimbabwe. Unfortunately, what we have seen is we have seen continued partisan statements from leaders of the security forces that obviously raise additional concerns.

It should be noted that the report from President Zuma cited the same concerns and called for a public code of conduct for the security forces because of those partisan statements by the military leadership. We have seen and we reported in May that the Zimbabwe Armed Forces have expanded their deployment nationwide, particularly into swing provinces, Manicaland and Masvingo, for legitimate, on the face of it, purposes: food distribution, disaster preparedness, and carrying out research on the army's history during independence. There is some concern that the message is intimidation.

I would just simply say, given the time, that what we have argued is that what needs to be done at this point is the United States—the United States Government—needs to clearly support SADC on insisting that the reforms that they have laid out are put into place in order to allow Zimbabwe to step back from a political abyss, which we see is threatening internal violence, regional instability, and a needless return to international isolation.

That is why our answer to your question of what the United States should do is support SADC in all possible ways, to insist on the minimal redlines a credible electoral process, urge SADC to deploy as early as possible a nationwide monitoring and observation network that covers electoral infrastructure, electoral security, ideally embedding SADC police with Zimbabwe police, and electoral participation. If SADC needs additional resources to complete its mission, we would hope that the United States would respond appropriately.

And finally, the United States should publicly indicate that it is willing, once credible and peaceful elections are held, to cooperate with the new government that comes into being through an election that's judged by all sides to be credible, transparent, and peaceful.

Thank you, Mr. Chairman.

[The prepared statement of Mr. Schneider follows:]

PREPARED STATEMENT OF MARK L. SCHNEIDER

I would like to express my appreciation to the chairman, Senator Christopher Coons, ranking member, Senator Jeff Flake, and members of the Africa Subcommittee of the Senate Foreign Relations Committee for the opportunity to testify this morning and for focusing attention on a looming electoral crisis in Zimbabwe.

Crisis Group is an independent, nonpartisan, nongovernmental organization that provides field-based analysis, policy advice, and recommendations to governments, the United Nations, the European Union and other multilateral organizations on the prevention and resolution of deadly conflict. Crisis Group was founded in 1995 by distinguished diplomats, statesmen, and opinion leaders including Career Ambassador Mort Abramowitz, Nobel Prize winner and former Finnish President, Martti Ahtisaari, late Congressman Stephen Solarz, and former U.N. and British diplomat, Mark Malloch-Brown.

Ambassador Thomas Pickering is our current chairman. Louise Arbour, former chief prosecutor at the International Criminal Tribunals for Rwanda and for the former Yugoslavia, and former U.N. High Commissioner for Human Rights, is our current president. In 2011, Crisis Group was awarded the Eisenhower Medal for Leadership and Service.

Crisis Group publishes some 80 reports and briefing papers annually, as well as a monthly CrisisWatch bulletin. Our staff is located on the ground in 10 regional offices, and 16 other locations, covering between them over 60 countries and focused on conflict prevention and post-conflict peace-building. We maintain advocacy and research offices in Brussels (our global headquarters), Washington, and New York. We have liaison offices in London, Beijing, and Moscow.

Crisis Group's Johannesburg-based southern Africa project has for some time been focused on the dismal state of governance, deterioration in human rights, and worsening economic and political conditions in Zimbabwe. In March 2008, we published a preelectoral report entitled ''Prospects from a Flawed Election.'' Hopefully a similar unhappy result will not reoccur.

Since the 2008 crisis, we have published nine reports on the post-electoral process in Zimbabwe, analyzing the negotiations, the Global Political Agreement (GPA) and the Southern Africa Development Community's (SADC) role in helping the country chart a reform roadmap to elections and a democratic transition. As the coalition government and transition Parliament's terms come to an end under the GPA on 29 June, instead of consensus and compromise, we see confrontation and conflict.

For the first time since that coalition government was formed, President Robert Mugabe issued a Presidential decree last Thursday that short-circuits the democratic process, by-passing the still functioning Parliament, cutting short voter registration, overriding constitutional provisions on time-lines for candidate nominations and posing obstacles to critical reforms that are essential not only to achieve fair and free elections but to achieve peaceful, credible, and transparent elections. The playing field—as we concluded in our 6 May report ''Zimbabwe: Election Scenarios'' and our analysts reaffirmed recently in Harare—is far from level.

Over the weekend, SADC heads of state met as the oversight and monitoring authority of compliance with the GPA and received a report from its current facilitator, South African President Jacob Zuma. The report underscored the GPA commitment that ''elections shall be held under conditions where all parties shall participate freely, on equal footing, in an environment free of intimidation and violent; and that this is necessary in order to bring into being the next government which shall enjoy undisputed credibility.''

We strongly agree with those views.

President Zuma reported on actions related to the pending harmonised elections with a clearly critical message that resulted in SADC issuing warnings to Zimbabwe regarding compliance with the previously negotiated GPA electoral roadmap. SADC essentially called for important reforms to be in place before elections are held and also urged the government to request the Constitutional Court to delay its call for elections prior to 31 July to permit compliance with current constitutional electoral provisions and enable key reforms to be adopted. The 31 July date, the Zuma report stated ''is fraught with legal contestation, political dispute and heightened tensions. . . .''

Among the reforms discussed in President Zuma's report which were endorsed in the SADC communique were the following, many of which touch on concerns that we also have raised:

- Media reforms;
- The rule of law (which explicitly refers to security concerns regarding military and intelligence interference in the elections which would be in violation of Section 208 of the new Constitution);
- The role of the Joint Monitoring and Implementation Committee (JOMIC);
- Electoral date, Validity of Electoral Regulations; and
- Deployment of SADC elections observers.

We remain hopeful that SADC will continue to insist on those reforms and convince not only President Mugabe but all parties to step back from a political abyss that threatens internal violence, regional instability and a needless return to international isolation.

The shortest possible response to ''What should the United States Government do at this critical moment?'' Mr. Chairman, is simply this: Support SADC in all possible ways to insist that the minimal ''redlines'' be adhered to for a credible presidential, parliamentary and local election.

SADC will hopefully quickly open an office in Harare and establish a nationwide monitoring apparatus covering electoral infrastructure, electoral security, and electoral participation. Where those basic reforms are agreed, the U.S. can offer whatever technical, financial and other assistance that might be needed. In addition, the U.S. should reiterate its readiness to cooperate with a new government if chosen in an election that is judged by all sides in Zimbabwe and SADC to be transparent, peaceful, and credible.

Where we stand: The clock is running now on what may be 6 weeks until a hastily called election in a country that suffered widespread, brutal national violence during and following its last flawed and discredited election in 2008.

In the wake of the 31 May court ruling that elections must be held before 31 July, the focus inside and outside Zimbabwe is whether there is any way to avoid a repeat of the undemocratic and violent 2008 elections. We believe that there still are options that include a pragmatic political consensus on delaying for several months—but not later than 29 October—the actual date, and getting court concurrence. President Mugabe's disputed decree setting 31 July as the election date also would have to be modified. However, additional time is clearly needed to permit the implementation of basic reforms to avoid a repeat of the 2008 disaster. His subsequent Executive order making a series of amendments to electoral law that shorten registration, nomination, and campaign periods also has drawn opposition charges of unconstitutionality.

The new constitution provides that the current 30-day voter registration period be completed, a process that would take to 9 July. It also provides that the Nomination Court sit for 14 days thereafter for candidates to register and be accepted and then allows for a minimum of 30 days campaigning, which cannot feasibly occur by 31 July.

At this stage, there is:

- No agreed and final registration roll;
- No electoral law approved by Parliament;
- No candidates formally nominated or approved for President or for 358 seats in Parliament;
- No time for a campaign after candidates are named;

- Little time for ballots to be printed;
- Less time for ballots to be distributed to 9,449 polling stations;
- No testing of electronic tabulation processes;
- No agreement for domestic electoral monitoring;
- No authorization for international electoral monitoring; and
- No transparent indication of how the election will be funded.

Behind the procedural and legal issues, there are critical unresolved political issues that complicate the current election that Crisis Group outlined in its last report: Within the Zimbabwe African National Union-Patriotic Front (ZANU–PF), ''hardliner'' and ''reformist'' camps are fighting over who will succeed 89-year-old President Robert Mugabe in the future. The opposition, the Movement for Democratic Change (MDC–T) led by Prime Minister Morgan Tsvangirai is struggling with infighting and limited capacity to mobilise its supporters, let alone to find avenues for electoral cooperation with the other MDC faction, which itself is divided. Some officers high in the security and intelligence forces seem unwilling to contemplate a possible opposition win and their rhetoric and increased deployment in swing provinces constitute intimidation.

The way forward also requires a clear understanding of the unfulfilled elements within the GPA that would help lay foundations for normalizing political processes and, by extension, foster conditions for free and fair elections. Unfortunately, the GPA was treated as a ''cease-fire'' document and as a framework for further negotiation, rather than as a formal agreement to be implemented. Despite a new constitution, this central drawback remains largely unchanged as resistance to reform continues to characterise the country's uneven power-sharing arrangement. The two uneasy party partners in that coalition government are President Robert Mugabe and ZANU–PF; and the wings of the Movement for Democratic Change, the MDC–T of Prime Minister Tsvangirai and the remaining MDC faction. An election roadmap was drawn up in July 2011, but key areas of disagreement relating to elections, the media, security environment, and institutional partisanship have not been adequately addressed.

There are also profound concerns that an election outcome that results in ZANU–PF losing power will not be respected by powerful elements in the security forces. Many military and intelligence officers articulate partisan political preferences under the guise of defending the gains of Zimbabwe's national democratic revolution. They even have described the MDC partners in government, particularly MDC–T and its leader, Morgan Tsvangirai, as national (and regional) security threats. Such dangerous rhetoric has yet to be countermanded by President Mugabe, the commander in chief of the country's defense force.

There have been some reforms put in place, highlighted by the adoption of a new constitution endorsed by over 95 percent of Zimbabweans who participated in the 16 March referendum. The replacement of the much criticized independence/Lancaster House constitution has both substantive and symbolic value. It was critical in the GPA and pressed by the Southern Africa Development Community (SADC), which monitors the GPA. However, its passage has had virtually no immediate or direct impact yet on achieving ''free and fair'' conditions for the elections.

An overview of key reform concerns and what may be possible in a restricted timeframe to help build toward a credible election process and outcome remains pertinent.

Three major goals called for under the GPA have yet to be achieved:

    (i) An end to state sponsored violence;

    (ii) Security sector reform; and

    (iii) Formation of adequately funded, credible, independent electoral authorities.

With respect to these goals, key reforms promised in the draft election roadmap that was signed in July 2011 by all GPA participants have been blocked. With respect to the integrity of the electoral process, the key reforms are aimed at:

    (i) Access to information;

    (ii) Freedom to participate; and

    (iii) Safety and security.

All require urgent attention;

1. ACCESS TO INFORMATION

Media and the State Broadcaster: The media environment remains distorted and partisan. The State broadcaster (TV and especially radio) remains the primary source of information for most Zimbabweans. Largely hostile to MDC formations (especially MDC–T), it is unashamedly partisan to ZANU–PF. The new commercial

FM radio stations Star FM and Zi-FM have provided limited alternative voices but even here their ownership underscores a ZANU–PF bias.

ZANU–PF continues to point to "pirate radio stations" and "independent" print media as evidence of "balance" and progress toward a "free media." External radio and local independent newspapers, however, have a very limited footprint compared to the state broadcaster. Consequently the media environment is severely prejudiced against parties other than ZANU–PF.

The Minister of Information and Publicity should urgently instruct state media (both electronic and print media) to: ensure balanced and objective reporting; provide reasonably equal access; desist from publishing and broadcasting hate speech; accept paid advertisements from all political parties; and also provide priority access to the Zimbabwe Electoral Commission (ZEC) for public service voter education announcements. Instructions should be public to rebuild public confidence in State media and foster citizen accountability for media freedom.

Longer term concerns regarding regulation and partisan governance of the media, including amending restrictive provisions of the Access to Information and Protection of Privacy Act (AIPPA) and Public Order and Security Act (POSA), were to be part of the reform agenda and at least must be addressed in the post-election environment, and commitment to address these concerns should be secured by all parties.

Extension of Voter Education: The ZEC must accredit more civil society organisations to undertake voter education about new election rules, regulations, and procedures, including how to access the voters roll, how to check for accuracy and where to file complaints. The ZEC should proactively enable civil society organisations, including faith-based networks to disseminate information about the forthcoming elections, processes, and institutions. The ZEC should also direct the Zimbabwe Republic Police (ZRP) to stop interfering with civil society groups who disseminate information about elections and election processes. Continued harassment of those involved in voter education effectively criminalizes the exercise of basic democratic rights, undermines public trust in election and consolidates concerns that the ZRP is pursuing a partisan political agenda.

2. FREEDOM TO PARTICIPATE

Citizen Verification of Voter Registration and an Audit of Voters Roll: No voters roll is perfect, but in Zimbabwe there have been widespread and well-founded concerns that the roll has been used as a tool to manipulate participation and exclusion. According to the ZEC in April, the Registrar General had registered 60,000 new voters and removed 345,000 deceased persons since December 2012. Yet there are continuing concerns of over and under registration that only credible auditing of the rolls can remedy. Since the April–May 21-day registration process, another 200,000 voters were reported added yielding an estimated but highly questionable total of 5.87 million. Political parties sharply criticised the differing standards, hours, resources available to register voters in different constituencies and a seeming surfeit of opportunities in ZANU–PF areas and far fewer in areas seen as favoring MDC. A new 30-day voter registration drive that started on Monday 10 June must address the shortfalls and anomalies identified in the May process. Anecdotal feedback during the first week suggests, however, that many problems remain.

The current final registration process which should last for 30 days now is being cut short by Presidential order to 17 days. Assuring that a final roll including all eligible voters is prepared and available is not a simple task—and with voters able to vote in any ward in their electoral district the potential for fraud rises considerably.

The integrity of the voters roll would be vastly enhanced by a full ZEC supervised audit of the existing roll. This could be done in a short timeframe and resources with resources already available through external EU funders. If SADC requested additional funding to support an independent audit, we would urge the U.S. to support such an effort.

Beyond the parties, the public should be provided with a reasonable time and opportunity to check the voter roll and effective methods to correct all flaws, particularly those that exclude citizens from voting.

Utilisation of Social Media: The ZEC and Registrar General must improve from their performances during the May registration drive when neither advertised any details on their respective Web sites. They need to take advantage of social media and the Internet to communicate the location of mobile voter registration stations, their hours and days of operation, registration procedures, required documentation, appeal mechanisms and their right to be registered should they meet all prerequisites.

The integrity of the voting process itself must include particular attention to the early/special voting process for elections, estimated to be some 100,000, to ensure concerns about multiple voting are minimised and if possible totally eradicated.

Reporting Election Results: It seems unlikely that ZEC will have the necessary technical infrastructure in place to ensure electronic reconciliation of voters roll for early voters or even on election day. In addition the ZEC does not have equipment for transmission of polling station results which will mean a reliance on Zimbabwe Republic Police communication equipment. At the very least, public details on the processes that will be followed should be made available to avoid as far as possible misapprehensions and distrust. The full tabulation and reporting process should be monitored by SADC observers.

Political Campaigning: Conditions must be ensured for the promotion of free political activity across the country. Each party must actively promote political tolerance and be seen to be doing so. There should be widespread dissemination of the political parties' code of conduct (during elections) by the parties themselves, but also through civil society and democracy supporting institutions. A remedial infrastructure to address any violations must be functioning and accessible.

Party Code of Conduct: Given the existing polarization, and taking into account the 2008 election dispute, all parties, especially those in the GPA, must consent and sign a code of conduct, with SADC as witness. The code should be widely disseminated and commit parties to promote political tolerance, reject any use of violence by their members (with threat of expulsion from the party for any who engage in those acts), and agree to settle any election outcome dispute through the formal channels ultimately outlined in the Electoral Act. Its compliance should be monitored by ZEC, the Zimbabwe Human Rights Commission and if passed and functioning, the "Special Investigation Committee" provided for in the draft Electoral Act, as well as by SADC.

Developing early warning and rapid response capacities: Zimbabwean parties should put in place early warning and rapid response mechanisms to deal with issues of violence and intimidation as a matter of urgency. A reconfiguration of the existing Joint Monitoring and Implementation Committee (JOMIC) structure presents the most realistic institutional option, but again requires political will and SADC support.

Strengthening Monitoring and Observation: An early SADC observation and monitoring mechanism must be put in place in compliance with the recommendations of the Democracy and Electoral Assistance Unit (DEAU) of the African Union, which in 2012 noted the need for African elections to transform toward long-term observation. Ideally, SADC observers and monitors must be in place at least 60 days before elections; now, they should be urgently deployed. Funding to underwrite a meaningful monitoring and observer footprint should be assured, and in addition to EU funding support to SADC, the U.S. should be prepared to respond urgently to any requests.

In addition, observers should be drawn from a range of other countries. ZANU–PF's control over the Foreign Ministry already has seen rejection of proposals from countries which have current sanctions on Zimbabwe, such as the U.S. Hopefully that will change. But there are other countries with good democratic credentials who should be encouraged to apply.

3. SAFETY AND SECURITY

Issues of political violence and allegations of partisanship within Zimbabwe's security services have been effectively side-stepped during the life of the GPA. Although wide-scale political violence has remained at a low level, it is worth remembering that the situation in February and March 2008 was also peaceful. Understanding how violence manifests in Zimbabwe requires a more sophisticated analysis of its characteristics and the infrastructure that services it. Despite mitigating interventions to promote reconciliation and conflict resolution in many communities across Zimbabwe, the infrastructure of repression remains largely in place. The "politics of fear" continues to harvest on the legacy of abuse, institutional bias, and systemic impunity. Even over recent months, there have been serious instances of harassment and intimidation against civil society activists and opposition political leaders particularly in rural communities. The absence of a visible deterrent or effective remedy to further abuse is a significant factor in the current environment.

Equally worrisome has been a recent expansion of deployment of the Zimbawe National Army, which we detailed in our May report, for what appear to be worthy public purposes such as food distribution, disaster response preparation and a so-called army history of independence. The concentration of those deployments in political swing provinces such as Manicaland and Masvingo raises concerns.

Security sector reform has been deadlocked by ZANU–PF opposition, despite calls for "security sector realignment" from SADC. There is substantial fear that security forces could take actions to undermine the campaigns and serious concern that they will not remain neutral as election results are being tabulated. The continued push for a credible and transparent election process by domestic and regional civil society and political figures, requires a diplomatic strategy to address these electoral and post-electoral security sector concerns.

The legacy of mistrust—the centrality of the Zimbabwe Republic Police: Zimbabwe has a long history of election related violence and intimidation. This history is compounded by systemic levels of impunity. Consequently, many ZRP perpetrators continue to live within the same communities where abuses occurred. While the police are only identified as perpetrators in a minority of cases, there are widespread allegations that they failed to protect citizens under attack or to adequately investigate political violence. It should be noted that the vast majority of people subject to politically related abuse between 2008 and 2012 have not reported these matters to the police. Details on over 12,000 cases covering this period were submitted in September 2012 to JOMIC facilitation team. In over 90 percent of these cases, the matter was not reported to the police by the victims. The police hierarchy has compounded concerns by demonstrating clear political partisanship in favour of ZANU–PF. Evidence in this regard is incontrovertible.

As with other aspects of Security Sector Reform, concerns about the police require a long-term strategy. There are, however, critical actions in the short term that can be taken to enhance the election environment and raise general levels of confidence.

- Deployment of SADC police officers as an "African solution to an African problem" to work with their ZRP counterparts prior to, during, and after elections. Rules of engagement for fellow SADC officers can ensure there is no untoward interference, but they must be mandated to report to SADC monitoring and observation structures.
- Detail should also be provided of ZRP command structures, including names and contact details of commanders and their respective geographical responsibilities under the electoral security plan.
- A security sector code of conduct should be in place before the elections, coupled with a public commitment made to this code by the security force chiefs and all rank and file members. This would be greatly enhanced if it was done in response to an order from the President, as current Commander in Chief. In addition, and in light of ongoing concerns about the partisan role of the military, they, along with the Central Intelligence Organisation (CIO) should be confined to barracks during the campaigning period as a sign of good will and an investment in building confidence amongst the general population.

CONCLUSION

The uncontested constitutional referendum in March enabled Zimbabweans to participate in a voting process without fear of retribution. The pending parliamentary and Presidential balloting is another matter. SADC remains the point vehicle for pressing for conditions on the ground to allow for credible elections and a process with integrity, including adequate domestic and international monitoring of all aspects of the process. The U.S. should support those efforts.

Senator COONS. Thank you, Mr. Schneider.
Mr. Moss.

STATEMENT OF TODD MOSS, PH.D., VICE PRESIDENT FOR PROGRAMS AND SENIOR FELLOW, CENTER FOR GLOBAL DEVELOPMENT, WASHINGTON, DC

Mr. MOSS. Thank you, Chairman Coons, Ranking Member Flake. Robert Mugabe, after 33 years in power, will soon be running for yet another term. This hearing is a timely opportunity to shape United States policy, not only because Zimbabwe is facing a critical moment, but also because I am increasingly concerned that our government may be sleepwalking down the wrong path.

We are at serious risk of sending the wrong signals and damaging U.S. interests in the region. This danger is especially high while the Assistant Secretary position remains vacant.

Let me start with three analytical points. First, I believe it is already far too late for a free and fair election in 2013. The ZANU–PF intimidation machine has been running full steam for the past 5 years. Local party bosses know who the opposition sympathizers are, in some cases even going door to door and marking houses. The police have repeatedly raided civic groups. Even radios, the principal way most Zimbabweans get news, have been banned and confiscated in many rural areas. Imagine the chilling effect of banning radios in a rural area.

As a result of the systematic campaign of fear already in place, we should not be surprised if the actual election day passes peaceably. We should thus severely discount the relevance of observers that just fly in and declare voting calm and orderly.

Second, even if Mr. Mugabe somehow loses, ZANU–PF will not allow Morgan Tsvangirai to become President. We know this because it has already happened. In 2008 Mr. Mugabe lost the first round. While he was surprised at this defeat, he was prepared to step down, but the military convinced him to stay and promised him that they would ensure his victory in a second round, and indeed they did.

Under the direction of senior army officers, party militias attacked the MDC's supporters and the nation's civil society networks. At least 80 people were killed, hundreds went missing, thousands were injured, and hundreds of thousands of Zimbabweans were driven from their homes.

There is no reason whatsoever for us to believe that in 2013 this will be any different. Mr. Mugabe will simply not step down if he loses. So if the outcome is already decided, then it cannot by definition be a competitive election.

In fact, the election itself is not an expression of democratic will, nor a process for Zimbabwe to select a political leader. It is in reality a form of political theater, only grudgingly tolerated by Mr. Mugabe. If we focus on the minor details, the deep weeds of the electoral process, like the current wrestling over the election date or the length of the registration process, I fear we will miss this bigger picture.

Third, Zimbabwe's economic collapse has been halted, but reports of a broad recovery are premature. The end of hyperinflation and the modest bounceback are welcome, but these are also the predictable result of dropping a worthless local currency and moving to the U.S. dollar. The Finance Minister, Tendai Biti, has done a very impressive job under grim conditions, but the foundation for full economic turnaround is still missing.

Also missing are hundreds of millions of dollars in diamond revenues controlled by ZANU–PF and the military. Instead of paying for Zimbabwe's reconstruction, the country's diamonds are funding the repression machine.

So what does this all mean for U.S. policy? I will quickly offer three suggestions. First, the United States should become more active and creative on Zimbabwe policy. Zimbabwe does not want to remain a pariah state, a fact that we should be able to leverage. This need not cost blood or treasure. It does mean working in a nuanced and resourceful manner with like-minded allies to find opportunities to increase political and economic freedom. When necessary, we should deploy the full capabilities of the U.S. Government, including and beyond the State Department.

Second, we absolutely should not endorse an election whose outcome is already known, nor should we prematurely normalize relations. Engagement and flexibility does not mean appeasement. The absence of wide-scale violence is not the same as a credible election. Until the signs of true political reform are clear, we should keep in place our current travel and financial sanctions against those responsible for violence and political repression.

Similarly, the United States should resist any premature efforts to clear Zimbabwe's arrears at the international financial institutions. Recall, if you will, that the Zimbabwe Democratic and Economic Recovery Act became U.S. law in 2001 and was cosponsored by Senators Bill Frist, Jesse Helms, Joe Biden, Hillary Clinton, and Russ Feingold. The act's conditions for reengagement are still appropriate today. These include restoration of the rule of law, freedom of speech and association, and an end to violence and intimidation. I am worried that our government may be sending premature signals that these have been restored when they most certainly have not.

Finally, the United States should prepare for real change in Zimbabwe. Despite my short-term pessimism, I am optimistic about Zimbabwe's long-term future and for building a fruitful partnership with the United States. We should be actively seeking dialogue with potential future leaders, planning for quick-reacting forms of recovery assistance, and finding ways of aiding democratic forces.

To conclude, Zimbabwe has fallen off the U.S. foreign policy agenda just at the time that the rest of Africa is booming and becoming an important partner for the United States. If we are seen as accepting a sham election, it will damage America's reputation at just the time we should be standing on principle. We may have limited policy tools to influence events in Zimbabwe, but it is in our long-term interests to help encourage the country to turn away from the hatred and fear of the past and toward a new Zimbabwe based on openness, prosperity, and freedom.

Thank you.

[The prepared statement of Mr. Moss follows:]

PREPARED STATEMENT OF DR. TODD J. MOSS

Thank you, Chairman Coons, Ranking Member Flake, and other members of the subcommittee. I appreciate that the subcommittee is holding a hearing on the economic and political challenges in Zimbabwe. I proudly served in the State Department of the previous administration, but did not work directly on Zimbabwe policy. Nevertheless, I have been actively involved with the country for more than two decades and now lead the Center for Global Development's work on Zimbabwe.

After 33 years in power, Robert Mugabe is running for yet another term. To put this in perspective, jump forward to the year 2041 and imagine that President Obama is still President, has deployed the FBI, CIA, and U.S. Marines to crush his domestic opponents, and is then running again for another term. Unthinkable? That's the situation in Zimbabwe today.

This is therefore a timely opportunity to shape U.S. policy, not only because Zimbabwe is facing a critical juncture, but also because I am increasingly concerned our government may be sleepwalking down the wrong path. Before making recommendations for U.S. policy, let me make three analytical points.

First, it is already far too late for a free and fair election in 2013. The window for a truly competitive election reflecting the will of the people has long closed. The ZANU–PF machine of intimidation has been, over the past 4 years, methodically ensuring the outcome of the next election. Local party bosses are well aware of who might be sympathizers for the Movement for Democratic Change (MDC), including going door to door and marking houses. If the past is any guide, they also have contingency plans in place for deploying armed groups if necessary. The arrest and unlawful detention of human rights lawyer Beatrice Mtetwa in March was only the most well-known incident of government repression. Civic organizations, especially those involved in electoral education (e.g., the Zimbabwe Electoral Support Network) and victims' assistance (e.g., the Counseling Services Unit, The Zimbabwe Peace Project) have been especially targeted. A list of arrests and raids on civic groups over just the past 10 months, compiled by researchers at the Robert F. Kennedy Center for Justice and Human Rights (Appendix A), paints a chilling portrait of a government afraid of its own people and willing to take extraordinary efforts to suppress their views.[1]

The Government of Zimbabwe has even taken the highly unusual step of confiscating all radios in many rural areas, where most of the population lives. Radios are the principal way most Zimbabweans get news—and yet they are banned. As a result of the systematic campaign of fear and intimidation that is already in place, we should not be surprised if the actual election day passes peaceably. Thus, we should severely discount the relevance of observers that fly in a few days prior and then declare voting is calm and mostly orderly. I would be surprised if it was otherwise.

Second, even if Mr. Mugabe somehow loses, ZANU–PF will not allow Morgan Tsvangirai to become President. I am confident in this assessment because we have already seen how ZANU–PF responds when they lose. In the March 29, 2008, vote, Mr. Mugabe lost the first round. There are credible reports, including excellent Washington Post reporting (Appendix B), that Mr. Mugabe was surprised at his defeat but prepared to accept the will of the people and to step down. However, the military leadership, desperate to protect their insider privileges, convinced Mr. Mugabe that he should instead compete in a second round and that they would ensure his victory. Indeed they did. ZANU–PF militias, under the direction of senior army officers, attacked the MDC's supporters and civil society networks. By the time of the second round 3 months later, at least 80 people were dead, hundreds missing, thousands injured, and hundreds of thousands driven from their homes. The violence against ordinary citizens was so severe that Mr. Tsvangirai sought refuge in a foreign embassy and was forced to withdraw from the race to spare further death and destruction. There is no reason whatsoever to believe that 2013 will be any different. Mr. Mugabe will not step down if he loses again. Thus, if the outcome is already decided, then it cannot, by definition, be a free and fair election.

Third, Zimbabwe's economic collapse has been halted but reports of a broad recovery are premature. It is true that hyperinflation and a worthless local currency are both gone, enabling some modest bounce back. This is the predictable result of dropping the Zimbabwe dollar and moving to a currency system based on the U.S. dollar. These are positive steps to be sure, and the Finance Minister Tendai Biti has done an impressive job managing the country's finances under grim conditions. Mr. Biti has also begun responsible first steps toward reengagement with the international financial institutions. But the foundation for a full economic turnaround—which requires restoration of private property rights, security of contracts, and protection of individual rights of association—are sorely missing.[2] In the World Bank's Doing Business indicators, Zimbabwe is still ranked near the global bottom, at 172nd out of 185 countries. Most tellingly, the Zimbabwean professional and working classes have continued to vote with their feet by leaving the country in droves and staying abroad. (The millions of Zimbabwean citizens in South Africa and elsewhere abroad who are denied their right to vote is another factor that will sway the outcome.)

Also missing from the recovery are the hundreds of millions of dollars in diamond revenues that should be in the Zimbabwean Treasury. According to credible reporting from groups like Partnership Africa Canada and Global Witness, Zimbabwe's diamonds are tightly controlled by a web of corrupt and secretive business networks linked to ZANU–PF and the country's military.[3] Instead of paying for teachers or stocking health clinics, Zimbabwe's diamonds are funding the repression machine.

What does this all mean for U.S. policy? I offer three suggestions.

First, the United States should become more active and creative on Zimbabwe policy than has been the case for the past 4 years. If we hope to help shape events in that part of the world, we cannot continue to be passive bystanders. Neither can a superpower that believes in democracy wash its hands of a country just because the options are all challenging. Instead we should actively engage with our allies, with Zimbabwe's neighbors, and, when appropriate, with Zimbabwe's political and civic leaders. Zimbabwe does not want to remain a pariah state, a fact that we should leverage. This means working in a nuanced and resourceful manner to find opportunities to increase political and economic freedom for Zimbabweans by working with others that share our goals and, when necessary, deploying the full capabilities of the U.S. Government, including and beyond the State Department.

One important caveat to emphasize is that we should not expect South Africa, the regional power, to be much help. Despite its own proud history of fighting oppression, the Government of South Africa has, for a variety of reasons, shown little willingness to support democratic forces in Zimbabwe and has instead too often been willing to look the other way when horrific abuses have taken place under its nose. After repeated attempts by American officials to try to sway South Africa, it should be clear that this is a losing strategy.

Second, we should not endorse an election whose outcome is already known nor should we prematurely lower our guard on sanctions or aid. Engagement and flexibility does not mean appeasement. The administration should be wary of rash declarations of success and should view the 2013 Presidential election within the context of the broader environment for the free expression of political beliefs, not just a one-day exercise in political theater under the watchful eye of the security forces. The absence of wide scale violence is not the same as a credible election or a signal that it is time to normalize relations. We should, until the signs of true political reform are clear, keep in place our current travel and financial sanctions against those responsible for violence and political repression. Those who argue for sanctions to be lifted now have not yet made a convincing case for how removal would credibly help the democratic process. Similarly, until we have confidence that change is real, the U.S. should resist any premature efforts to clear Zimbabwe's arrears at the World Bank and other international financial institutions, which would be a step toward significant new lending to the country.[4] The conditions for reengagement outlined in the Zimbabwe Democracy and Economic Recovery Act are still apt. Recall if you will that ZDERA became U.S. law in 2001 and was cosponsored by Senators Bill Frist, Jesse Helms, Joe Biden, Hillary Clinton, and Russ Feingold.

Finally, the U.S. should prepare for real change. Even though I am pessimistic about the chances of immediate political change, I am optimistic about Zimbabwe's long-term future. Zimbabwe's elderly political class cannot be in power forever. A new generation, including within ZANU–PF, longs for Zimbabwe to return to the community of nations and finally reap the bounty of its natural wealth and abundant human capital. The U.S. should be actively seeking dialogue with potential future leaders, planning for quick-reacting forms of recovery assistance, and finding ways of aiding democratic forces.[5]

Zimbabwe has fallen off the U.S. foreign policy agenda just as the rest of Africa is booming economically and becoming an important partner for the United States. The southern African region cannot thrive while Zimbabwe remains an outlier. We may have few good options and limited policy tools, but it is still in the long-term interests of the United States to help encourage Zimbabwe to turn away from the hatred and fear of the past and toward a new Zimbabwe based on openness, prosperity, and freedom.

End Notes

[1] See also "Pattern of Suppression in Zimbabwe a Concern for RFK Center," Robert F. Kennedy Center for Justice and Human Rights, April 2, 2013.
[2] Michael Clemens and Todd Moss, "Costs and Causes of Zimbabwe's Crisis," CGD Brief, 2005.
[3] "Reap What You Sow: Greed and Corruption in Zimbabwe's Marange Diamond Fields," Partnership Africa Canada, November 2012; "Zimbabwe's diamond sector and EU restrictive measures," Global Witness, January 2013; "Financing a Parallel Government? The involvement of the secret police and military in Zimbabwe's diamond, cotton and property sectors," Global Witness, June 2012.
[4] Benjamin Leo and Todd Moss, "Moving Mugabe's Mountain: Zimbabwe's Path to Arrears Clearance and Debt Relief," CGD Working Paper 190, 2009.
[5] Todd Moss and Stewart Patrick, "The Day After Comrade Bob: Applying Post-Conflict Reconstruction Lessons to Zimbabwe," CGD Working Paper 72, 2005.

[EDITOR'S NOTE.—Appendixes A and B mentioned above can be found in the "Additional Material Submitted for the Record" section at the end of the hearing.]

Senator COONS. Well, thank you, Mr. Moss, Mr. Schneider, Mr. Mahvinga.

Mr. Moss, if I might, you offer in some ways the most bracing and broad summary of what I think is a common theme across all five witnesses today, which is grave concern that should elections be held on an accelerated timeline there is virtually no chance that they will be peaceful, free, fair, effective, respectable, certifiable.

You urge that the United States become more active and creative on Zimbabwe policy, yet also recognize we have relatively limited policy tools. I would agree with your assertion that we should not be lifting sanctions simply in response to a peaceful election, but should instead insist on the whole menu of respect for private property, for human rights, for open civil society, for free media, as well as the precondition of being a free and fair election.

How would you suggest we go about being more innovative, more active, more creative on Zimbabwe policy? What else would you urge us to do?

Mr. MOSS. Thank you for the question. I think it is not just a matter of engaging or not engaging, lifting sanctions or not lifting sanctions. The United States can be a very creative and powerful actor. It can be a player if we are actively engaged, and it can be a player if there is direction given to the administration from above or from Congress to try to achieve a particular outcome.

What I fear I have seen, particularly over the last 4 years, is a stepping back of the United States, where they are frustrated that sanctions have not led to the outcome that we may desire and that our policy tools are limited, so we become passive actors and in a sense we outsource our foreign policy to SADC or sometimes to the South Africans, which may have very different outcomes in mind. And while on paper we may share some of the very same interests, we do not always behave in the same manner.

So I believe that the United States, through various components of the U.S. Government, if it was given clear direction on what the United States was trying to achieve, could come up with much more creative strategies to try to, for instance, peel away part of ZANU–PF with which we will have to work with in the future, and try to further isolate parts of ZANU–PF with which we should not work with in the future. I think that kind of nudge could make an important difference, not just in Zimbabwe, but internationally, where we have seen a general stepping back, including among our European and other allies, which have also gotten frustrated with Zimbabwe.

Senator COONS. Thank you.

Mr. Schneider, ICG's recent report also indicates MDC–T and ZANU–PF may be internally fragmented. This is not unusual for long-standing contestants for political parties that are created more around an individual than around a policy agenda, but do you see this as a sign of the emergence of more pragmatic or reformist leaders within these groups, or is it just a sign of ongoing competition for the spoils of power?

Mr. SCHNEIDER. Within some of those factions, clearly there is a pragmatic effort to move forward. I think they recognize that Zimbabwe is sort of poised on the edge of a cliff and it is either going to go over that cliff and see further violence, further disaster, or move away from it and hopefully build a different kind of future.

I will say that right now, at least within ZANU–PF, it is the minority of those who have expressed those kinds of views, but I do think we should try to find ways to work with them as well as those within MDCT that are ready to respect the constitution, respect the rule of law, and abide by the clear conditions that are required in order to have a free, fair, election and then to move forward on the reforms that remain to be achieved.

There are a series of reforms on removing the repressive provisions on the media law, on security, that have not taken place. Those need to take place. There needs to be far more done with respect to ending impunity for violations of the law, violations of human rights.

I will say one thing. The constitution that was adopted was adopted as a result of compromise between the two major political parties and with the support generally of civil society. That provided for the transitional election, not July 31, but within 4 months and that, as we have heard, by the end of October. And to the degree that we can press—and that is what we should be focused on right now: How do we move all of our diplomatic resources along with SADC and the AU in trying to bring about the conditions, and particularly control over the security forces, the conditions to permit that election to take place and the transition to occur?

It is clear, election day is not the crucial issue. The crucial issue is what happens before and after and ensuring respect for the outcome, particularly if it is an opposition outcome, is a critical part of the process.

Senator COONS. Mr. Schneider, do you think it is still possible for there to be elections within this calendar year if pushed back by several months, if all those preconditions are met? The referendum that approved the constitution, was broadly welcomed as being peaceful, with a high participation rate. But as you comment, it was because there was agreement between the political parties on the outcome.

Mr. Moss describes the likely outcome here as a, I think, barely tolerated political charade if it remains on the compressed schedule, but raises some question as to whether there can be a credible election in 2013 at all. Do you think it is still possible if SADC, AU, and other players like the United States align their resources, and if wings of both key political parties embrace the possibility of a positive path forward here?

Mr. SCHNEIDER. The answer is one hopes so. One cannot be confident, but I think that you have a much better chance of having that outcome if everybody is focused on those reforms and clearly sets them out as, these are the redlines, these are the benchmarks. Without these, there cannot be anything that is viewed as a credible election, even if it is peaceful on election day. And we still do not see that in place, and that is what we have raised in all of our reporting.

Senator COONS. Mr. Mahvinga, if I might, for all three of you and across many different sources, a key concern is security sector reform, the politicization of the police and the military and the lack of confidence that they will remain neutral in the election. What players inside or outside of Zimbabwe, in your view, have the credibility or resolve to successfully press for security sector reform, and is the security sector challenge, including the ongoing politicization of the security forces, really one of leadership or is it deeply entrenched in the security forces at all levels?

Mr. MAHVINGA. Thank you, Mr. Chairman. For Zimbabwe, the major challenge is one of the leadership of the security forces, which is extremely partisan and highly politicized. So focus should really be on ensuring that the leadership are reined in to conduct themselves in a politically neutral way.

Within Zimbabwe, President Mugabe as the Commander in Chief of the defense forces has that political power to rein the security forces in. For the U.S. Government, the best way would be to work through and support SADC initiatives. South Africa as the facilitator for Zimbabwe is best placed within the framework of the roadmap to elections to put forward a code of conduct for the security forces to comply with and to ensure that there are mechanisms to enforce it. The challenge has been a failure to enforce the laws.

The new constitution that was signed into law last month has a provision in article 208 that all security force should be nonpartisan, politically neutral, and should not align themselves with any one political party. So it is just a matter of ensuring that there are mechanisms to implement this article that already is agreed to by all the political parties.

Senator COONS. Thank you, Mr. Mahvinga.

Senator Flake.

Senator FLAKE. Thank you.

Let me follow up on a question Chairman Coons asked. Mr. Schneider, you seemed to indicate that you believe that free and fair elections could be held still this year if it is put off a bit. Mr. Moss, you say not this year. Mr. Moss, do you want to explain why that is the case, why a couple more months would not do it?

Mr. MOSS. Yes, thank you. I think we want to differentiate between the mechanics and the legal provisions for holding an election. Clearly you want to try to follow—you want to follow the letter of the law to the extent you can. You obviously want to have the ballots where they are supposed to be, so that the mechanics operate as they should. Actually, USAID has an extremely long and proud history of supporting these technical preparations for elections, including in the 2008 elections in Zimbabwe. Support there was essential to getting to that first round loss for ZANU–PF and actually seeing what had happened.

Senator FLAKE. Just one second. On that first round loss, then, your feeling was the technical aspects there, were there sufficient ballots distributed in the rural areas? All of the technical things were there for the first election?

Mr. MOSS. To the best of my knowledge, yes. But we want to separate the mechanics of an election from the environment for people to use that election to express their political preferences. Here we have to go back even before 2008, but certainly 2008 was a watershed area where towns, villages, regions that had voted in the first round election for the opposition provided a map for the security forces to know where to target. They then executed this plan of intimidation to ensure that this next round and no future elections would ever be lost to the ruling party.

That system, intense intimidation and organized violence, including I have no doubt in my mind that there are contingency plans in place for armed groups to be deployed if necessary—and people know that. Once you have had your house burned down, you have had a family member disappear, maybe you have had a family member chased out of the country, and you have been told that, we know how you vote, you are going to think twice before expressing your political—and they have taken your radio away. You are going to think twice about voting for who you really want to vote for.

I do not believe in that environment, even if it is technically capable, it is technically correct, that you are going to see the true expression of the Zimbabwean people.

Senator FLAKE. You have outlined in your written testimony a series of abuses that have occurred just over the past little while. Is it your feeling that that is laying the groundwork, obviously with the intimidation factor, but that they are readying a plan to make sure that they do not go through what they had to go through last time? Is that an accurate assessment?

Mr. MOSS. That is very accurate. You know, I do not think that it is an accident that the groups involved in electoral education have been specifically targeted. In my written testimony I submitted a list from the Robert F. Kennedy Center for Human Rights and Justice and I think that fits into a larger pattern of the security forces working closely with the ruling party to ensure the electoral outcome that they desire.

Senator FLAKE. Mr. Schneider, you mentioned that it would be useful if SADC forces were embedded with Zimbabwean security forces. How likely is it that ZANU–PF would allow that?

Mr. SCHNEIDER. It is an interesting question. SADC has done this in other countries and that is a kind of—when you read what they are asking for in terms of deployment with respect to security, that would be a way to carry out what they are saying needs to be done. That is, observation of the security forces by SADC monitors. We urge that that be done and at least be proposed as a way to try and avoid—first, reducing the politics of fear; and second, actually avoiding, hopefully, violence during the electoral and post-electoral process.

Let me just say one other thing. I have always believed that the United States and others on the outside should listen very carefully to people on the inside. So it does seem to me when trying to reach judgment whether or not it is worthwhile taking the risk of going forward with elections, we need to be sure that we are listening to civil society groups inside Zimbabwe, the church, and other non-governmental organizations, as well as the opposition political parties, the ones who are going to put their lives on the line to be candidates, to run for office, to campaign, to go out and vote. So we should be listening to them in coming to a judgment about whether or not we should support the process.

The other point I would make is that one of the things that does give us concern as well, which I hope would be reversed, is the government rejected the permission for the U.N. elections needs assessment mission to enter the country. U.N. elections is part of the technical operations that essentially say, this is what you need in order to carry out the elections, this is what it costs, et cetera. It is something that still needs to be done and I think would give confidence to others that at least if these standards are met at least the technical side of things would be covered.

But I agree with Tom in the sense that the fundamental issue is are there going to be pressures, political and otherwise, so that the security forces feel that they cannot do what they did in 2008.

Senator FLAKE. Mr. Mahvinga, how significant is it that the AU has stepped forward now and will monitor? Is that likely to have more of an impact on the ZANU–PF's thinking than SADC or other international organizations?

Mr. MAHVINGA. There are challenges with the statement from the African Union on deploying long-term observers to Zimbabwe. The first is that it appears to endorse the idea that elections should happen by end of July. So that is likely to strengthen ZANU–PF's resolve to move ahead because the AU is saying now we are moving in to observe. We have wanted to a see a situation where there is a clear position to insist on the reforms that must take place ahead of elections, which the AU simply has not addressed.

It also appears to be bringing tension between SADC and the AU, because the SADC leadership has said there is need to extend the date for elections and to look at the minimum conditions for free and fair elections, particularly the role of the security forces, before, during, and after the elections.

Senator FLAKE. You sound as if the AU is almost acting as an enabler for this. Is that your assessment? Mr. Moss, you seem to be nodding your head there.

Mr. MOSS. I think there is certainly a risk there, especially if we are focused on the technical observation of the conduct of the elections rather than the broader political environment. I do not know if they are accurate, but certainly comments by the AU chair this morning would seem to say that the problems over the electoral schedule were up to Zimbabweans to resolve, the AU was not going to get involved, does not suggest to me—if they are accurate—does not suggest to me a very active role for the AU.

The AU, I should add, has come a very, very long way in standing up against coups and standing on principle against coups. They have a much tougher time standing up to a sitting head of state that may be behaving in a way worse than coupmakers.

Senator FLAKE. Thank you, Mr. Chairman.

Senator COONS. If you have any closing questions, feel free to ask them now.

Senator FLAKE. No, thank you.

Senator COONS. If I might, first Mr. Moss. The question that I asked previously of Ambassador Yamamoto about diamond revenues: What measures do you believe can and should be taken to ensure that diamond revenues are not being diverted and misused? I believe in your testimony you suggest that you believe this is in part financing the ZANU–PF intimidation machine. Should the United States press for Zimbabwe's expulsion from the KP, from the Kimberley Process, seek to engage it in the EITI, the Extractive Industries Transparency Initiative? Or is there some other credible, creative path forward for ensuring transparency in this vital sector that is likely generating hundreds of millions of dollars that are currently unaccounted for?

Mr. MOSS. Yes, thank you. There is some very good research on the Zimbabwean diamond sector from Partnership Africa, Canada, and from Global Witness that are both footnoted in my written testimony. I would urge anyone looking for details to turn there for evidence of the problem.

What is clearly happening is that diamonds are being taken directly out of the country. They are controlled by a secret network of businesses, likely linked to the military forces. What we do know is that the revenues from those diamonds are for the most part not going into the Treasury where they belong. I think it is reasonable to assume that if it is going to the military then that is also being used as a parallel, almost a parallel government to run the security forces and intelligence services.

The Kimberley Process itself is not set up to deal with human rights abuses or to deal with theft of mineral revenues. It was set up principally to try to squeeze so-called conflict diamonds out of the global supply chain. It did a pretty good job at that. I am sympathetic to those within the KP that think that this is a bridge too far and that the KP is not set up to deal with this problem.

EITI would be helpful, but EITI is entirely a voluntary organization. So the Government of Zimbabwe would have to volunteer to release information on where its diamond revenues are going. I think that is extremely unlikely.

I do think that the United States could use its diplomatic and other influence, particularly working with our like-minded allies, to try to squeeze the diamond centers that are purchasing these diamonds and enabling the violence and repression in Zimbabwe quite directly. But I do not have a simple off-the-shelf answer for—and there's no simple mechanism that exists now to do that.

Senator COONS. You mentioned, in response to a question from Senator Flake and in your previous testimony, some skepticism about just how far South Africa is willing to go in order to press for fundamental reform in order to ensure not just a peaceful election, but a truly free and fair and open election. What other regional partners, what other regional allies, what other leaders in SADC, might we be looking to to help insist that Zimbabwe upholds the SADC principles in its conduct of the upcoming election?

Mr. MOSS. There are other members within SADC which I think are more willing to be forward-leaning on Zimbabwe. Unfortunately, they are much smaller and less influential than South Africa. Some of the other bigger players have very long historical links with ZANU–PF and are much less likely to try to influence them.

I think it was a terrible accident of history that President Mwanawasa, who had been leading the charge before his death, the SADC pressure sort of evaporated after his death.

What is striking to me when I look at the entire African Continent is that you would think that southern Africa should be the region driving the continent politically, economically, diplomatically, and it is just not the case. East and West Africa are much further ahead in democratic reforms, in pushing for sound economic policies. I actually think we could get more leverage in working with countries like Ghana, like Nigeria, like Tanzania, to try to encourage a broader African stand against what I think everybody recognizes is a disaster in Zimbabwe. And everyone is just sort of waiting for the President to die to move to that next phase.

But I think that a lot of the region would like to try to push it and not just sit back and wait for that event.

Senator COONS. My last question for you, if I might. On this panel you have sort of pressed hard on a view that we should not simply wait, we should not simply accept peaceful elections; we should be using all the levers available to us. Others have suggested it is important for us to convey an openness to reducing sanctions on Zimbabwe should there be progress.

Would you suggest strengthening or tightening sanctions? Are there tools that the United States unilaterally can deploy in the event that the very bad outcome you are predicting comes to pass?

Mr. MOSS. Yes. I think that we can do both. We are absolutely correct to continually review and reduce or take people off the sanctions list when they are no longer becoming a problem, and we should make it very clear that we are willing to do that when there are appropriate actions taken on the other side.

At the same time, there are areas where the United States could be looking to further squeeze and tighten those recalcitrant elements within the government, particularly if there is a bad election or a violence-driven election result that either rejects an opposition victory or enforces a noncredible win by certain parties.

One example could be preemptive contract sanctions, which is a tool that exists out there. It has not been deployed yet. What that would mean is that the United States, working with the Treasury, working with some of our allies in Europe, could make, if Zimbabwe blows up, could make a preemptive statement that future loans or contracts signed by an illegitimate Zimbabwe Government would not be enforceable in United States courts. That could have a chilling effect not only on United States and European foreign investment, obviously, but could also have a chilling effect on investment from places like Russia and China.

Senator COONS. Interesting.

If I could, Mr. Schneider, the International Crisis Group's recent report concludes that, if I read this right, it may be the best way forward to prepare for a plan for further power-sharing. Is ICG suggesting a managed democracy approach is better than a truly failed outcome, than a military rejection of an electoral outcome that is suspect at best? And does this put at risk short-circuiting the popular will of Zimbabweans?

Mr. SCHNEIDER. What we were essentially saying is if there is, in fact, no movement toward setting the ground for an adequate electoral process, that you have to think what then do you do. It is in that context, an extension of the transition government in some way. But the answer is, at least at this stage, still to focus on the reforms required so that there are conditions for, at the very least, a peaceful, credible election, and then as much pressure as is possible on the security forces to accept the outcome where it goes against the ZANU–PF.

I should make one other point. The diamonds issue is part of the security problem in Zimbabwe. The information that we had in one of our reports a while ago indicated that Zimbabwe Defense Industries, which is an army-owned company, holds a 40-percent stake in the Anjin diamond mine operation. The Minister of Finance at the time, Tendai Biti, noted that, where the estimate was about $500 million in revenues from diamonds, that the state Treasury received only about 10 percent.

So there is clearly mechanisms there and an interest on the part of the security forces not to see the situation changed in this regard, and there have to be efforts made to put additional pressure on where they act in a way that violates the constitution and prevents a democratic expression of the voters from being realized.

Senator COONS. Mr. Mahvinga, if I might, Ambassador Andrew Young recently met with President Mugabe at the suggestion of the administration and was accompanied by the U.S. Ambassador. The U.S. Ambassador has also accompanied Jesse Jackson to a meeting with President Mugabe. How is this engagement viewed by Zimbabwean civil society? What have you heard in your recent visits in terms of how the United States outreach or recent efforts has been received?

Mr. MAHVINGA. There has been concern that perhaps that kind of engagement is premature, given the conditions on the ground, and that there is really need for the U.S. Government now to be supporting processes toward credible elections that lead to a peaceful transfer to the government-elect, and that really focuses and supports to civil society groups at two levels, the first level being financial support for their activities, election activities within the country, but also increasing pressure through SADC and other players to ensure that there is no harassment and intimidation and the beatings that we have been witnessing in the recent months of civil society groups.

So there is a real concern that perhaps the U.S. Government should closely look at what is happening on the ground, closely look at the whole of the security forces and ensure that its action position toward Zimbabwe is in response to clear improvements on the ground and not just incentives that are not related to progress and reforms achieved.

Senator COONS. Thank you, Mr. Mahvinga.

Senator Flake, did you have any further questions?

Senator FLAKE. No, thank you.

Senator COONS. Let me, if I might, thank you, Mr. Moss, Mr. Schneider, Mr. Mahvinga. We will be consulting afterward. Obviously, President Obama is about to take his first trip to the region with an impending trip to South Africa. I think there is still the possibility of progress in security sector reform, in electoral reform, and with some significant changes it is still possible for there to be credible, free, and fair elections later this year.

But we are clearly at a tipping point. All five of our witnesses today have drawn in sharp terms the grave concerns that the United States should have and the hesitancy we should have toward lifting any sanctions prematurely and the redoubling of effort that is required with our regional partners and our diplomatic efforts to ensure that we do not lose this opportunity for progress in Zimbabwe.

So we will leave the record open for a week for other members of the committee who may have wanted to be with us but were at another event that was happening at the same time. I want to thank all the members of our second panel and all of our witnesses today for your engagement and for your determination, for your insight.

With that, this hearing is adjourned.

[Whereupon, at 11:43 a.m., the hearing was adjourned.]

ADDITIONAL MATERIAL SUBMITTED FOR THE RECORD

TWO ARTICLES SUBMITTED BY TODD MOSS AS ATTACHMENTS TO
HIS PREPARED STATEMENT

APPENDIX A

ARRESTS & RAIDS OF CIVIC GROUPS IN ZIMBABWE (AUG. 2012–MAY 2013)

Source: Robert F. Kennedy Center for Justice and Human Rights

- On April 23, Advocacy Officer Trevor Murai, with Student's Solidarity Trust, was arrested and detained after making a presentation on elections during a workshop organized by the Christian Alliance. Under the amended Electoral Act of 2012, "voter education," strictly understood, can only proceed under the authority of the Zimbabwe Electoral Commission (ZEC), a body that is staffed by President Mugabe and ZANU–PF loyalists.
- Beatrice Mtetwa, Zimbabwe's most prominent human rights lawyer—and founding board member of Zimbabwe Lawyer's for Human Rights (ZLHR)—was arrested on Sunday, March 17, for allegedly "obstructing" the police as they raided an office of the Movement for Democratic Change (MDC) without a warrant. Beatrice was transferred to the notorious Rhodesville Prison in Harare, kept in solitary confinement, and consistently denied access to family members despite a court ruling that ordered her release. African, regional, and international human rights groups denounced the "alarming" and "unlawful" arrest.

    Æ State prosecutors during the week of April 8 served Mtetwa's attorneys with the new allegations together with court papers to prepare for her trial, which has been set for the May 27–31 at the Harare Magistrates Court. Mtetwa faces 20 allegations by the State in its criminal case against her in what has been described as a "desperate act of "embellishment.""

- Radio Dialogue, a popular community radio station in Bulawayo, was raided by police and officers from the Central Intelligence Organization (CIO) on March 1. Police allegedly confiscated 180 shortwave radios and later broke into the director's personal residence looking for similar devices. The director, Zenzele Ndbele was interrogated by police for several hours, later released, and asked to appear before a magistrate the following Monday. In another report, police allegedly went door to door in Gandanzara, Ward 23 of Makoni South in search of radios. The "ban" on radios was announced on February 19 by Assistant Police Commissioner Charity Charamba, who claimed that the radios would be used to "communicate hate speech" ahead of the constitutional referendum and elections.
- On Tuesday, February 19, the headquarters of the Zimbabwe Electoral Support Network (ZESN) were raided by police, breaking down the organization's main security gate in the process. During the same day, the ZESN regional office in Masvingo was also broken into by unknown individuals, but largely believed to be the work of the police and related security forces. Much like the February 11 raid of the ZPP offices, police came armed with a warrant in search of "subversive material." On February 21, the ZESN Masvingo offices were broken into again; their security guard reported that armed persons "entered the premises and broke a window, taking the field officer's desk drawers which included over 800 T-shirts, power adapters, and a blackberry phone.
- On Monday, February 11, plain-clothed police officers raided the Hillside offices of the Zimbabwe Peace Project (ZPP), which documents instances of police misconduct, human rights abuses, and political violence across the country. Police claimed to have a warrant for "illegal entry of goods, persons or communications equipment." According to several reports, police confiscated ZPP's violence incidence reports, as well as upwards of 60 phones and 60 wind-up radios that are frequently used by ZPP staff during grassroots outreach activities. Police returned again that night, demanding entry into the director's office. ZPP is led by Jestina Mukoko, a former newscaster and prominent human rights activist who, in December 2008, was abducted, tortured, and held incommunicado for nearly a month.

    Æ The police vendetta against Jestina Mukoko escalated in early March. The national police commissioner, Augustine Chihuri, stated on national television his intent to detain Mukoko and requested the public's help in "tracking her down." Mukoko presented herself before the state authorities on Friday, March 8, where she was formally charged with "running an unregistered organization," "smuggling radio sets and mobile phones," and "broadcasting without a license."

- Also on February 11, police raided the offices of the Community Tolerance, Reconciliation, and Development Group (COTRAD) and the National Association of Nongovernmental Organizations (NANGO), one the largest civil society coalition groups in Zimbabwe. Two people were reportedly arrested during these raids.
- On February 6, 2013, police once again raided the Bulawayo offices of the National Youth Development Trust (NYDT) on the grounds that the group was in possession of "subversive material" and for allegedly "conducting illegal voter registration activities." The raid came two days after two other members from NYDT were arrested in Lupane after being found in possession of voter registration receipts. The police initially detained 40 people affiliated with NYDT, but were later released.

    Æ On April 10, 2013, three NYDT members were arrested in Bulawayo for mobilizing residents in Pumula to register as voters. NYDT was implementing a plan whereby the urged residents with Econet phone lines to register using their SIM card receipts, which contains proof of where they reside.

- On January 14, 2013, Okay Machisa, director of the Zimbabwe Human Rights Association (ZimRights) was arrested and charged with conspiracy to commit [voter registration] fraud, forgery, and publishing falsehoods. This arrest followed the December 2012 arrest of another high-ranking ZimRights employee, Leo Chamahwinya, also for allegedly conducting "illegal voter registration" activities. Three other individuals who are not ZimRights employees have been implicated in the case as well, and have been repeatedly denied bail and access to lawyers.
- In December, two officials from the Zimbabwe Electoral Support Network (ZESN) were detained for organizing an "unsanctioned public meeting" on International Human Rights Day. The same afternoon, two leaders of the Zimbabwe Congress of Trade Unions (ZCTU), the largest grouping of trade union activists in the country, were briefly arrested in Bulawayo as they attempted to march in the city center.
- Several employees from the Counseling Services Unit (CSU)—a nonprofit organization that provides support to victims of torture and political violence—were arrested and illegally detained in November because CSU was allegedly in possession of "offensive and subversive material." The three individuals were eventually charged with causing "malicious damage to property" in contravention of Section 140 of the Criminal Law (Codification and Reform) Act, 4 days after their arrest.
- In October 2012, Nkosilathi Moyo, director of the Zimbabwe Organization for Youth in Politics (ZOYP), was convicted under POSA for organizing a civic education workshop without getting "permission" from the police. Police disrupted the workshop and arrested Nkosilathi, along with Maureen Gombakomba and Beloved Chiweshe from the Crisis in Zimbabwe Coalition. The Crisis officials were cleared and released the same day but Moyo was detained, charged, and ultimately found guilty by a Kwekwe magistrate. He received a 12-month jail sentence. Six months were suspended with a $500 fine, on condition that he not commit the same crime again for the next 5 years.
- In September, police arrested 10 members of Women of Zimbabwe Arise (WOZA) during a peaceful protest and again during a November 13 altercation during which police officers verbally referenced the Gukurahundi massacres and ordered WOZA members to not speak in their native Ndebele language. National Coordinator Jenni Williams and Programs Coordinator Magodonga Mahlangu were arrested and later released without charge. On December 11, upwards of 80 WOZA members were again arrested, physically assaulted, and detained at Bulawayo Central police station for staging a peaceful protest about the deteriorating water situation in the city. Most recently, during a peaceful protest on February 13, police assaulted and arrested nine WOZA members, including Jenni Williams. WOZA members filed an official complaint due to the harsh treatment they received, and all members were later released without charge.
- A life skills workshop organized by the National Youth Development Trust (NYDT) was barred from taking place in September without legitimate reason from the local police, the second such instance in less than a month when an

event was illegally dispersed. On both occasions, NYDT employees were detained, questioned, and later harassed by local authorities.

- On September 28, the president of the Zimbabwe National Students Union (ZINASU) was arrested, along with three colleagues, for organizing and an ''illegal demonstration.'' The four individuals were denied access to food, lawyers, and their respective family members for extended periods of time.
- In August, the headquarters of the Gay and Lesbian Alliance of Zimbabwe (GALZ) was ransacked on multiple occasions, during which visibly drunk riot police assaulted GALZ employees and illegally seized office materials. Authorities later attempted to shut down GALZ operations altogether, charging a co-chairperson with running an ''unregistered'' organization, the same rationale used to arrest and detain the director of the Zimbabwe Human Rights NGO Forum the previous month.

———

APPENDIX B

[From the Washington Post, July 5, 2008]

INSIDE MUGABE'S VIOLENT CRACKDOWN NOTES, WITNESSES DETAIL HOW CAMPAIGN WAS CONCEIVED AND EXECUTED BY LEADER, AIDES

(By Craig Timberg)

HARARE, Zimbabwe.—President Robert Mugabe summoned his top security officials to a government training center near his rural home in central Zimbabwe on the afternoon of March 30. In a voice barely audible at first, he informed the leaders of the state security apparatus that had enforced his rule for 28 years that he had lost the presidential vote held the previous day.

Then Mugabe told the gathering he planned to give up power in a televised speech to the nation the next day, according to the written notes of one participant that were corroborated by two other people with direct knowledge of the meeting.

But Zimbabwe's military chief, Gen. Constantine Chiwenga, responded that the choice was not Mugabe's alone to make. According to two firsthand accounts of the meeting, Chiwenga told Mugabe his military would take control of the country to keep him in office or the president could contest a runoff election, directed in the field by senior army officers supervising a military-style campaign against the opposition.

Mugabe, the only leader this country has known since its break from white rule nearly three decades ago, agreed to remain in the race and rely on the army to ensure his victory. During an April 8 military planning meeting, according to written notes and the accounts of participants, the plan was given a code name: CIBD. The acronym, which proved apt in the fevered campaign that unfolded over the following weeks, stood for: Coercion. Intimidation. Beating. Displacement.

In the three months between the March 29 vote and the June 27 runoff election, ruling-party militias under the guidance of 200 senior army officers battered the Movement for Democratic Change, bringing the opposition party's network of activists to the verge of oblivion. By election day, more than 80 opposition supporters were dead, hundreds were missing, thousands were injured and hundreds of thousands were homeless. Morgan Tsvangirai, the party's leader, dropped out of the contest and took refuge in the Dutch Embassy.

This account reveals previously undisclosed details of the strategy behind the campaign as it was conceived and executed by Mugabe and his top advisers, who from that first meeting through the final vote appeared to hold decisive influence over the president.

The Washington Post was given access to the written record by a participant of several private meetings attended by Mugabe in the period between the first round of voting and the runoff election. The notes were corroborated by witnesses to the internal debates. Many of the people interviewed, including members of Mugabe's inner circle, spoke on the condition of anonymity for fear of government retribution. Much of the reporting for this article was conducted by a Zimbabwean reporter for The Post whose name is being withheld for security reasons.

What emerges from these accounts is a ruling inner circle that debated only in passing the consequences of the political violence on the country and on international opinion. Mugabe and his advisers also showed little concern in these meetings for the most basic rules of democracy that have taken hold in some other African nations born from anti-colonial independence movements.

Mugabe's party, the Zimbabwe African National Union-Patriotic Front, took power in 1980 after a protracted guerrilla war. The notes and interviews make clear that its military supporters, who stood to lose wealth and influence if Mugabe bowed out, were not prepared to relinquish their authority simply because voters checked Tsvangirai's name on the ballots.

"The small piece of paper cannot take the country," Solomon Mujuru, the former guerrilla commander who once headed Zimbabwe's military, told the party's ruling politburo on April 4, according to notes of the meeting and interviews with some of those who attended.

"Professional Killers"

The plan's first phase unfolded the week after the high-level meeting, as Mugabe supporters began erecting 2,000 party compounds across the country that would serve as bases for the party militias.

At first, the beatings with whips, striking with sticks, torture and other forms of intimidation appeared consistent with the country's past political violence. Little of it was fatal.

That changed May 5 in the remote farming village of Chaona, located 65 miles north of the capital, Harare. The village of dirt streets had voted for Tsvangirai in the election's first round after decades of supporting Mugabe.

On the evening of May 5—three days after Mugabe's government finally released the official results of the March 29 election—200 Mugabe supporters rampaged through its streets. By the time the militia finished, seven people were dead and the injured bore the hallmarks of a new kind of political violence.

Women were stripped and beaten so viciously that whole sections of flesh fell away from their buttocks. Many had to lie facedown in hospital beds during weeks of recovery. Men's genitals became targets. The official postmortem report on Chaona opposition activist Aleck Chiriseri listed crushed genitals among the causes of death. Other men died the same way.

At the funerals for Chiriseri and the others, opposition activists noted the gruesome condition of the corpses. Some in the crowds believed soldiers trained in torture were behind the killings, not the more improvisational ruling-party youth or liberation war veterans who traditionally served as Mugabe's enforcers.

"This is what alerted me that now we are dealing with professional killers," said Shepherd Mushonga, a top opposition leader for Mashonaland Central province, which includes Chaona.

Mushonga, a lawyer whose unlined face makes him look much younger than his 48 years, won a seat in parliament in the March vote on the strength of a village-by-village organization that Tsvangirai's party had worked hard to assemble in rural Mashonaland.

After Chaona, Mushonga turned that organization into a defense force for his own village, Kodzwa. Three dozen opposition activists, mostly men in their 20s and 30s, took shifts patrolling the village at night. The men armed themselves with sticks, shovels and axes small enough to slip into their pants pockets, Mushonga said.

The same militias that attacked Chaona worked their way gradually south through the rural district of Chiweshe, hitting Jingamvura, Bobo and, in the predawn hours of May 28, Kodzwa, where about 200 families live between two rivers.

When about 25 ruling-party militia members attempted to enter the village along its two dirt roads, Mushonga said, his patrols blew whistles, a prearranged signal for women, children and the elderly to flee south across one of the rivers to the relative safety of a neighboring village.

Over the next few hours, the two rival groups moved through Kodzwa's dark streets. Shortly after dawn, Mushonga's 46-year-old brother, Leonard, and about 10 other opposition activists cornered five of the ruling-party militia members. One of the militia members was armed with a bayonet, another a traditional club known as a knobkerrie.

In the scuffle, Leonard Mushonga and his group prevailed, beating the five intruders severely. But he said that this small, rare victory revealed evidence that elements of the army had been deployed against them.

One of the ruling-party men, Leonard Mushonga said, carried a military identification badge. In a police report on the incident, which led to the arrest of 26 opposition activists, the soldier was identified as Zacks Kanhukamwe, 47, a member of the Zimbabwe National Army. A second man, Petros Nyguwa, 45, was listed as a sergeant in the army.

He was also listed as a member of Mugabe's presidential guard.

Terror Brings Results

The death toll mounted through May, and almost all of the fatalities were opposition activists. Tsvangirai's personal advance man, Tonderai Ndira, 32, was abducted and killed. Police in riot gear raided opposition headquarters in Harare, arresting hundreds of families that had taken refuge there.

Even some of Mugabe's stalwarts grew uneasy, records of the meetings show.

Vice President Joice Mujuru, wife of former guerrilla commander Solomon Mujuru and a woman whose ferocity during the guerrilla war of the 1970s earned her the nickname Spill Blood, warned the ruling party's politburo in a May 14 meeting that the violence might backfire. Notes from that and other meetings, as well as interviews with participants, make clear that she was overruled repeatedly by Chiwenga, the military head, and by former security chief Emerson Mnangagwa.

Mnangagwa, 61, earned his nickname in the mid-1980s overseeing the so-called Gukurahundi, when a North Korea-trained army brigade slaughtered thousands of people in a southwestern region where Mugabe was unpopular. From then on, Mnangagwa was known as the Butcher of Matabeleland.

The ruling party turned to Mnangagwa to manage Mugabe's runoff campaign after first-round results, delayed for five weeks, showed Tsvangirai winning but not with the majority needed to avoid a second round.

The opposition, however, had won a clear parliamentary majority.

In private briefings to Mugabe's politburo, Mnangagwa expressed growing confidence that the violence was doing its job, according to records of the meetings. After Joice Mujuru raised concerns about the brutality in the May 14 meeting, Mnangagwa said only, ''Next agenda item,'' according to written notes and a party official who witnessed the exchange.

At a June 12 politburo meeting at party headquarters, Mnangagwa delivered another upbeat report.

According to one participant, he told the group that growing numbers of opposition activists in Mashonaland Central, Matabeleland North and parts of Masvingo province had been coerced into publicly renouncing their ties with Tsvangirai. Such events were usually held in the middle of the night, and featured the burning of opposition party cards and other regalia.

Talk within the ruling party began predicting a landslide victory in the runoff vote, less than three weeks away.

Mugabe's demeanor also brightened, said some of those who attended the meeting. Before it began, he joked with both Mnangagwa and Joice Mujuru.

It was the first time since the March vote, one party official recalled, that Mugabe laughed in public.

''Nothing to Go Back To''

The opposition's resistance in Chiweshe gradually withered under intensifying attacks by ruling-party militias. After the stalemate in Kodzwa, the militias continued moving south in June, finally reaching Manomano in the region's southwestern corner.

The opposition leader in Manomano was Gibbs Chironga, 44, who had won a seat in the local council as part of Tsvangirai's first-round landslide in the area. The Chirongas were shopkeepers with a busy store in Manomano. To defend that store, they kept a pair of shotguns on hand.

On June 20, a week before the runoff election, Mugabe's militias arrived in Manomano with an arsenal that had grown increasingly advanced as the vote approached.

Some carried AK–47 assault rifles, which are standard issue for Zimbabwe's army. For the attack on Manomano, witnesses counted six of the weapons.

About 150 militia members, some carrying the rifles, circled the Chironga family home. Gibbs Chironga fired warning shots from his shotgun, relatives and other witnesses recalled. Yet the militiamen kept coming. They broke open the ceiling with a barrage of rocks, then used hammers to batter down the walls.

When Gibbs Chironga emerged, a militia member shot him with an AK–47, said Hilton Chironga, his 41-year-old brother, who was wounded by gunfire. Gibbs died soon after.

His brother, sister and mother were beaten, then handcuffed and forced to drink a herbicide that burned their mouths and faces, relatives said.

Both Hilton Chironga and his 76-year-old mother, Nelia Chironga, were taken to the hospital in Harare, barely able to eat or speak. The whereabouts of Gibbs Chironga's sister remain unknown. The family home was burned to the ground.

''There's nothing to go back to at home,'' Hilton Chironga said softly, a bandage covering the wounds on his face and a pair of feeding tubes snaking into his nostrils.

''Even if I go back, they'll finish me off. That is what they want,'' he said.

Two days later, as Mugabe's militias intensified their attacks, Tsvangirai dropped out of the race.

Groups of ruling-party youths took over a field on the western edge of downtown Harare where he was attempting to have a rally, and soon after, he announced that the government's campaign of violence had made it impossible for him to continue. Privately, opposition officials said the party organization had been so damaged that they had no hope of winning the runoff vote.

On election day, Mugabe's militias drove voters to the polls and tracked through ballot serial numbers those who refused to vote or who cast ballots for Tsvangirai despite his boycott.

The 84-year-old leader took the oath of office two days later, for a sixth time. He waved a Bible in the air and exchanged congratulatory handshakes with Chiwenga, whose reelection plan he had adopted more than two months before, and the rest of his military leaders.

About the same time, a 29-year-old survivor of the first assault in Chaona, Patrick Mapondera, emerged from the hospital. His wife, who had also been badly beaten, was recovering from skin grafts to her buttocks. She could sit again.

Mapondera had been the opposition chairman for Chaona and several surrounding villages. If and when the couple returns home, he said, he does not expect to take up his job again.

''They've destroyed everything,'' he said.